Chapter 1

The day dawned dreary and grey. Rain pelted the windows like the pain battered my soul. It was evident that my lonely day was going to begin with hot tears streaming from my eyes again. Tears that I was now used to like an old familiar ache. The long ago past crept slowly into my conscious present. That daunting pain that I knew so well. Knew it well but without a welcoming thought. How could I stop the frightening memories from invading my life all over again?

Who could possibly even understand? So many frightening thoughts swirled in my mind and splashed into my soul. The darkness of it all peeled away the thin veneer of happiness I tried to portray in front of my family and the few friends I had. And I felt I could not trust any of them with the secrets that my life held. I knew of no path to lead me to salvation from the pain I had been enduring since the age of four.

Struggling through my routine if housecleaning, planning dinner, afternoon snacks for my children and pleading with God to deliver me from the atrocities of my childhood. I do not know if God ever heard my prayers. They had never been answered in over forty years. So, I doubted He ever heard.

Doubted He ever saw my tears and doubted He ever felt the aching in my heart.

Every day I continued weeping, vacuuming, dusting, all the normal things I so enjoyed doing for my family. But now, at his moment, it seemed more like sullen chores that reminded me that I was only meant to be an unhappy workhorse. Still, I enjoyed the routine in my own way because it was familiar and allowed me to make my home look new and shiny with the fresh lingering smells of cleansers. This was the only thing I took personal pride in. To me, my clean home meant I was worth being alive.

Relief came only when my laughing children bounded through the front door. All at once each one was telling me of their day at their respective schools while munching through bites of freshly baked cookies and between sips of hot chocolate. Suddenly I was happy. In fact, I was elated to have them home and relaying their adventures to me.

My weariness subsided as the love for my children took over me in waves that mere words cannot express. I never knew how to convey how happy they made me. How proud I was that they were mine. This is something that should have come naturally to me as a mother. But it did not work out that way for me. I only knew that when they spoke of their own adventures I felt as if nothing else in the world mattered.

So why could I not express that? Was there really that much anger, hatred, loneliness and walls of solitude in me so as to not allow me to be the decent mother I should be? My life was a big bundle of unanswered questions and doubts. And I had nowhere to turn to look for answers so I could feel secure in my position as a wife and mother. I was feeling desperate and trapped. More like a caged lion who had never tasted freedom. I pondered what freedom really meant or felt like.

Maybe it was fear that prevented me from being the mother that I should be. The mother I wanted to be but always fell short of accomplishing. Fear had always been my companion. Fear kept me from venturing out into an unknown abyss where I might get hurt or may never come back from. Fear is a quiet destroyer of confidence and self-esteem. It was fear that kept me from telling my husband about my past. He had no idea what kind of childhood I had been subjected to. I made up my mind to tell him because I so needed to talk to somebody, and I chose him to confide in.

When my husband came home later that evening, I tried to confide in him of the devastating incidents that haunted my mind on such days as this. But he was tired from work and dismissed any conversation with "Just write it down. I'll read it on my day off." His next day off was in three weeks. I could not wait that long.

The crushing memories invaded my life now, and in three weeks it would be even worse. I did not know what was happening to me and I was not really sure I wanted to know. It all seemed to be heading towards a doom I did not want to experience. I envisioned a hellish nightmare to be relived over again from my childhood.

So, on and on I wrote. And each time I felt wretched pain bubbling to the surface of my memories I ran for paper and pen. My fingers rushed to jot down the cataclysmic details of the scene before my mind's eye. And each time I wrote the appalling words connected with each scene I noticed that my heart grew lighter. Almost as if I was writing about a dear old friend that I pitied. A friend that was being saved from torture with each word that was written. I tried not to associate that dear friend as being in the same predicament as I was in. that would have been too much for my soul to handle. And yet, my heart ached for the torture that the little four-year-old girl was reliving. It was I who was reliving the nightmare for her.

In that way I could have the courage to write down what was happening in my mind's eye. As anyone knows the mind's eye sees with much more clarity what the heart tries to avoid. This is called keeping one's sanity. It is the basement of thoughts where you can store what cannot be faced at the time it is happening. My basement was full to capacity and was now spilling out of its confines. It had nowhere to go except to the forefront of my life. An when it invaded the present, it refused to go back where it came from. Once it tore through from the past, it no longer wanted to be left in the past to suffer alone. This misery needed company and it was not about to be ignored.

This was how the weeks went by. Household chores were interrupted by bouts of offensive whirling memories. Strangely enough whenever my children arrived home from school or were home on the weekends the invasion of memories dissipated. Life was happy and normal. At least for now it was normal. Memories and bad habits picked up along life's road are unpredictable. What is normal and acceptable to some seem outrageous and cruel to others. It depends on what you have been taught or what your beliefs are. The secret to keeping these memories at bay was to be surrounded by my children, they trusted me an depended on me. To love and protect them. They had no idea that I was living a double life of torment and anguish while I pretended to live a life of normality and happiness.

As promised, at the end of three weeks, my husband read all that I had written. Shocked and heartbroken at the revelations on each page he turned slowly to look at me. "Is this true? Did this really happen to you?"

I nodded and whispered "Yes. All of it. And it is those memories that make me cry on some days and feel scared on other days." I felt an enormous amount of relief that I was able to say it out loud and not carry this burden all alone.

"Why hadn't you told me before?" My husband choked back tears. His questions tumbled out almost as if they were one long question with several parts to it. His assessment of what he had just learned about me was that it was child abuse at its worst. He said it was incredulous that I had even survived those bloody beatings and strangulations. It occurred to him that the reason my voice was so high pitched was because of the many strangulations. He slowly continued with his next statements.

"This feels like I'm reading a book." He continued with a look of fear, pity and incredible anger for what I had been through as a child. "Divide it up and keep writing. I want to see how this all ends."

He had found it interesting enough that it reminded him of a book. He did not say it was like a book he had once read, only like it was written in the style that one finds in a book. These were the memories I had written as they came from the time, I was four years old but written as an abject adult full of misery. This was the beginning of my literary journey, although I did not realize it at that time. I was more involved in getting the memories out of my head and onto paper. And then out of my life for good. Even if I did not know the outcome of this adventure that lie ahead of me, I knew anything was better than keeping it bottled up inside me forever. It had to be let out. And it had to be soon.

The following week I busied myself with dividing up what I had written. As best as I could make out the different aspects of my horror, I soon realized that I could have the beginning of a manuscript. My husband was right. This sounded exactly like I was reading a book. I pondered the thought for a moment. Is this something that could possibly be publishable? How could it even benefit anyone knowing about my degrading background?

And as I continued to wonder, I began to think about how different my life would have been if someone had cared enough to advise me of life's cruelties and consequences. Maybe I could actually help someone in distress. I had never been anyone's saving grace, not even to myself, but there was still that lingering thought. The words of which to write to make people comprehend such a story scared me because I did not think of myself as a literary scholar. I was a bit on the shy side and did not have good communication skills. As a matter of fact, I had no real skills in life.

All the school of hard knocks had taught me was that I was not fit to be anything at all except a housekeeper. That was my one and only source of pride. My sisters were hoarders from a very young age while I loved to see things clean and shiny. I even went so far as to clean my eldest sister's house whenever I went to visit her. And I did it while singing and dancing.

I loved to listen to the radio as I went about polishing my furniture to a beautiful glossy shine, mopping the floors until they showed no signs of grime, and dancing to the music as I swept and vacuumed.

As the radio played on, I became immersed in the thought of another child or teenager having to experience the brutality at the hands of a person who was supposed to be a loving gentle caretaker. Either that be a friend or family member.

The music was interrupted by a guest speaker. This also caused me to interrupt my own thoughts. The guest speaker was a young man who professed to be a psychic. Psychics, or those who profess to be psychics, are not credible people in my opinion. They say only what they think you want to hear. And this gentleman was no exception.

"Now there's a bunch of hogwash wasting my music time. Hope he's not long winded." I said it out loud to no one. No such luck.

He dragged on and on and on and they soon took a station break. To my dismay he continued after the break. I was so disgusted with him that I actually called in to the radio station to tell them to put the music back on. He attempted to inform me that he could see me writing…successfully.

The next day while grocery shopping, I met a stranger who was picking up various snack food items. He stopped, stared at me then reluctantly said "I see you writing. Your story will be a best seller. It will even be a movie someday."

It was the radio psychic! His voice and accent were unmistakable. His sly grin did nothing to make me feel at ease with his statement. The intent looks in his eyes was unnerving, and I had to look away. This stranger seemed to be looking right through me and it chilled me to the bone. There was that fear factor that kept me from asking what he meant by that. I just turned and walked away as fast as I could from his presence.

Shaken, I left my cart of groceries right in the middle of the aisle and hurried out of the store. With no groceries to prepare a dinner meal with, this instantly became pizza night. For hours after I returned home, I sat thinking of my husband's words. "This feels like I'm reading a book."

And now this stranger's words "Your story will be a best seller." If someone has never been in this position it would be almost impossible to imagine the terror of the unknown can be. I could not get the stranger's words out of my mind.

What was God trying to tell me? This was not what I wanted at this time. I had a busy life already without worrying about what some person off the street, or off the radio, said to me.

After dropping off my children at school the next day I went to the local library to look up how to publish a manuscript. Instead, I came across book publishing companies. One such company, Doubleday Publishing, caught my attention. I liked the name but most important it was in New York. Clear across the United States. No one on the east coast would know me. While the west coast was filled with people and relatives who could easily identify me as the writer, the east coast was a safe place to be anonymous. I could stay in the background while possibly helping someone in need. Someone in dire circumstances who required that extra bit of courage to free themselves from whatever and whomever tormented their lives.

Flashes of anonymous faces having their bodies being whipped to a bloody pulp made my eyes tear up. I knew that feeling. I was one of them. Why could my parents not just whip me across my posterior? Why did the beatings have to be across almost every inch of my body? Time was running out. I had been in the library for the better part of the day. If I was going to do anything productive, I needed to hurry up and start making good solid decisions. But was I capable of doing that on my own? Perhaps. But then again, I never tried. This was going to be an interesting venture.

I took down all the necessary information to contact Doubleday Publishing, along with a few others, just in case Doubleday did not pan out. The next morning, I mailed off my manuscript, as I now referred to it, to Doubleday Publishing in New York. Then I waited and waited. Almost six weeks later I received my manuscript back.

My hands trembled as I expected the worse news possible. I braced myself. Glancing over each submitted page I saw nothing. No grammatical corrections. The only thing was a single red ink marking where one word was substituted out for another. Just one word out of all four chapters. The letter that accompanied my returned work announced that I had been assigned to an editor whom I could correspond with regarding my material. It was a standard letter of acknowledgement whereas the company informed me that they had received my submission.

In my unprofessional and untrained eye, there was nothing in it to inform me of much else, except that I would be contacted at a later unspecified date. I presumed it was unspecified just in case they changed their minds about contacting me. I decided to wait thirty days to see if Doubleday Publishing notified me of their decision. After that I would submit my writing to one of the other publishers on my list.

Several days later I received a phone call from a woman who introduced herself as "J.B.", an editor Doubleday Publishing. She wanted to discuss the future of my "book." In a blur I recall words such as "mesmerizing," "intriguing," "too graphic," but most of all "worthy of publication." Oh my gosh. She thought my writing was worth publishing.

Her soft tone of voice caught me by surprise because of the command of authority it carried. I repeated her name multiple times so I would not forget it. I wrote it down in different ways. "J.B., Jaybee, J.Bea, Jay B." one of them had to be right. There were several other spellings, but I felt one of these had to be the correct one. I would wait and see.

This first call was more perfunctory than anything else. A somewhat cursory conversation that did not involve much of a stand on what was about to happen to me within the next two years. I had not expected much but even so I thought she would be a little bit more thorough on what was to be expected of me. But here I sat, not knowing what the next step entailed. And furthermore, not even knowing what questions to ask. All I could do at this point was to write down whatever she said and try to make sense of it at a later date.

Without knowing it, this would become my ritual for almost the next two years. And because of it, I am now able to write about these conversations with J.B. and how our long-distance relationship developed into a solid friendship. As best as my memory serves me, the exact wording is used. When exact wording cannot be used, I express my feelings and or opinions as to what the conversations with J.B. were about. So, this first conversation, which led to dozens of other calls, was the cornerstone of all other calls. The one that was the basis for writing a successful manuscript. However, this all would turn out to be, I would forever remember this first time that I spoke to my gentle editor.

This was my introduction to the kind of brilliant editor that J.B. would, in time, become a friend that I trusted with my manuscript and with my life's secrets. The one person who transformed me into the courageous person who was able to write about a true horror story without any imagination. Without the talent of such other well- known writers of mystery and gore. Little did I know that she was to become much more than a mere run of the mill editor. She was more of a guiding light to me. And to the world, a great, kind, giving and humble human being.

Chapter 2

J.B.'s second call came approximately two weeks later. This was a first of many unexpected calls from her. There were never any set phone appointments throughout the entire time that we discussed the manuscript. Every call was random but appreciated. And each call was filled with advice from J.B., which I wrote down for future reference. I read then reread each page of notes so I could learn how to write as elegantly as J.B. spoke. As closely as I can remember, it went something like this:

"Hello M.S." She addressed me by my initials as my manuscript was signed that way. "This is J.B., I have thought about your work and have decided that, at this point in time, it has some sections that are way too graphic." I was stunned into silence as I feared she would deny my work at any moment. Whenever a person tries experimenting with something new, there is always that fear or doubt in whether or not you are suited for such a venture. At this time, this is exactly where I stood. Not knowing what else to do with my life, I was encouraged by J.B. to seek a life in the literary world.

"What exactly would I need to change to make it more presentable at this time?" I queried in a trembling voice. "I really do not want to change the tone of the story. It happened exactly as I have written it. The scenes, the language, all of it occurred just as it is written. I want it to be a truthful account of events." Here I was, a nobody, stating matter of factly what "I" wanted. I was ready to stand for what I felt was what the audience could comprehend and what I was ready to let the world know about my family and the way we functioned on a daily basis. But I was to learn that a seasoned author and editor knew more about getting a manuscript prepared for actual publication. I was way out of my league when it came to knowing how to go about doing that.

J.B. countered quickly, "Your factual accounts should never waver. Only the 'way' it is presented. Imagery is a very powerful thing and should be expressed as such when words cannot bring about the clarity of the statement."

I found her expression of vocabulary quite intriguing. So educated, so direct. J.B. could easily convey all the strengths and weaknesses of my work with her flair of understanding. That was it. She understood the ugliness of a tortured child, then caressed that child's pain with gentle words of encouragement. She paused while I pondered that thought, knowing that I would need those few moments to digest what she was saying.

After a few brief moments she continued in the same gentle tone. "These are events that go unreported in thousands of homes each year around the world. No doubt, if not exposed, could lead to a pandemic like proportions."

Meekly I whispered "I thought it was just me that went through such a dreadful childhood. Like it was my fault, as I had been told by my parents." This has been a lifelong journey for me of guilt and remorse for ever having even been born. And I did not know how to express these feeling to J.B.

"No, that is just simple fallacy. The mistaken belief that the child is at fault for the adult's cruelty. The tragedies that you reveal from your experiences will someday guide another person to freedom from their own mental, physical or emotional anguish."

J.B. held no judgement. Only optimism for a manuscript that she believed could bring comfort to someone else. "Write the way your heart feels as you remember each incident. Go to where your dark, hidden pain lies. And then awaken it so it can be released one final time."

There it was again. The eloquence of speech that I longed to possess. But in my own manner I asked "How do I find it? That hidden pain seems to find me, not the other way around. And it comes at the most inopportune times. "Will it hurt more if I go searching for it?"

Panic seized my throat and my already childlike voice pitched higher. So many years I had practiced speaking in the normal tone of an adult. But now my damaged vocal cords were threatening to surface in an uncontrolled falsetto stream. The more emotional I became, the more prevalent my damaged voice became, leaving me in a state of distress. It was a major embarrassment to be an adult with a child's voice. I hoped that J.B. understood the extent of injury my throat had sustained over the years from parental abuse.

Without making me feel as if she was belittling me for the questions I asked, J.B. instead comforted me in her soothing, soft voice. "That is exactly how you find it. It comes to you."

It finally reached me in a sudden jolt. No one writes about emotional instances in their lives. Emotions write themselves. Borne of loathsome insecurities, as tidal waves on an ocean crest. My mounting excitement left me breathless as I rushed through questions over questions. "How much time do I have to make the necessary corrections? Do I mail back the entire work or just the pages with the corrections? To whom should I address it to? How will I know when it has been written properly?" I still did not comprehend how to go about getting this new manuscript prepared for her next reading and editing. There were more questions that I cannot recall at the moment. The pouring out in such a way was pure desperation on my part in wanting to continue with the possibility of publishing my manuscript. I may have come across as desperate to J.B., but that is genuinely how I felt. A desperate person grasping at straws to accomplish the impossible. And this sweet-talking editor may just be the one person to help me see this through to the end. At least that was my hope.

"My dear," J.B. responded, take your time. You are not clocked into anyone's time demands. There is no contract, as yet. And if, and when, that time comes, I will confer with my trusted colleague on where to proceed from there. Mail back only the chapters that you feel needed extra work or corrections, along with your updated version. As far as the addressee, use the same business address but with 'Attention to J.B.O.' after the address."

An "O"? where did that come from? I surmised that J.B. were her first and middle initials, just as M.S. were mine. Not unusual and I gave it no further thought.

In a much lighter note, J.B. softly answered in an almost whimsical air. "Your heart will ache less and less with each revelation until only the memory of the pain will remain. There will be no active pain from there on." Such insight she had that it bordered on remarkable.

J.B. left me with the unshakable notion that she had also felt the stabbing pain of tragedy so severe that it left her heart scarred. A trauma so imbedded in her soul that she sounded wounded even to this day. But she did not elaborate on the details, so I did not probe for any. My selfish thoughts were focused on where this collaboration could take me. How it could benefit me and nobody else. There was soon a lesson for me to learn about how selfishness and gratitude cannot exist side by side. These were the kind of lessons one learns from familial ties and proper upbringing. These were also the things that I was not afforded while growing up. How I envied those who were brought up in such a way as to learn the simple lessons in life.

Ending the short conversation on this note, J.B. advised that I only write when the memories came naturally. "Do not try to push them to the forefront. And do not go looking for them. When the time is right, those long-forgotten memories will find you. That is the time to write. You need not ask if the timing is right. You will automatically know. And that timing will produce your best work. I hope this helps you achieve what you are working towards in your manuscript."

With excitement surging in my veins, I answered all too quickly that I would write again as soon as the memories of my youth found me. I vowed that I would not consciously go looking for them, for I knew where they were. And I would wait patiently for them to unlock the door and release themselves from the dark prison where I had banished them so long ago. I had never expected nor wanted them to ever escape from those dark recesses of my mind. But it was not a permanent solution. They had been creeping into my present life as intruding aliens. And I needed a solution on how to rid myself of them.

The mysterious editor who preferred to be known only by her initials, now addressed me by my own initials. I supposed that was only fair as I had initiated the interaction by signing my manuscript as M.S. I had done so to keep my gender in anonymity. This kept gender bias or preference at a minimum and equality at a maximum. I never gave it a second thought that someone would reciprocate by using their own initials as a counterbalance. I had much to learn about how to communicate with people. Especially very talented and educated people.

"When you make all the corrections you feel are needed, please send them back and I will read them then discuss them with my colleague, John Loring, for a possible book style. Until then, thank you for your interest in Doubleday Publishing. Goodbye." J.B. sounded cheerful and optimistic as we hung up from that conversation. She gave me hope when she said she would discuss my writing with her trusted colleague. But first I needed to whip up some more chapters and make necessary amendments to what I had already submitted. This was a hard conversation because I had no idea where to begin writing a true manuscript that was worthy of the accolades J.B. had bestowed upon me. But I would try my best to live up to her encouraging words.

After we hung up, I sat in awe of what had just transpired. The events leading up to this day appeared to be edging towards the eventual publishing of my manuscript. A manuscript that was meant to be an actual book. At no time in my life had I even had the notion of becoming a writer. I felt that was reserved for the educated mind with a flair for communication. My skills in that department were sorely depleted, if I ever even had any social skills to begin with. This was something I had to prove to myself before I could prove it to others. It was in the knowing how to even begin to prove that which was my roadblock. But to learn how to speak properly would be my first lesson in writing properly. I was at a crossroads and did not even recognize it. I screamed in my head for not learning how to speak in a cultured manner before this.

I blamed my parents for raising my siblings and myself in an area outside of town nicknamed Okie Flats. And yes, it was exactly how the name implies. And the customary speech in the area was nowhere near the caliber of a distinguished author type material.

Chapter 3

Fervently I wrote almost each day to accomplish what J.B. had advised in her comments as we conversed. Too graphic? Alright, I would leave out some of the vilest language that was hurled at me on a daily basis. I needed to convey my story without using exact language and without leaving out pertinent details, while still enhancing the situations described. No foul language, except where it was necessary to complete the visual thought.

Nowhere did I reveal a description so literal as to offend the reader. Yet, if someone was in the same or similar circumstance, they could easily recognize the dangers and respond in a positive manner. In doing so, someone's life could be spared of misery or even death. Their plight could then be redirected towards freedom from their predicament. Within the pages of this manuscript, they could find answers to the problems in their daily lives.

What I failed to foresee was that I had to fully relive each incident again before I could ease it into less graphic wording. Still keeping in mind J.B.'s warning that my vocabulary should stimulate the imagination. If someone can picture the actual events by reading words, then that makes for a successful story. What I did not reveal to J.B. was that I had no communication skills so therefore I could only tell the story as I remember it, in my own words, plain and simple. No eloquence. No sophistication. No educated speech or phrases.

After several attempts at correcting and revising the graphic areas of the manuscript, I felt the need to ask J.B. if I was headed in the right direction in accomplishing what she had instructed me on. So, I called the number she had given me and left a message for her to call back. Cell phones were not the norm back then, but landlines were the way of communication. Had it been several years into the future things might have been a lot easier for us to communicate. Until then it would have to suffice in leaving a message or relying on random calls.

When J.B. called back, I asked her "I would just like to address the composition I have rewritten." Wanting to get right to the meat of the subject, I read to her the chapter with the most corrections in it. As I read, I could see that this version was far better written than the original. J.B. let me know that she agreed with the changes I had made. She was always straightforward with her opinions on the subject at hand.

Slowly she answered "It is a very mesmerizing restructure indeed. You have done a magnificent job of formulating the basis of your story without losing the integrity of the interpretation. The essence of your message has remained intact while the offensiveness of expression has diminished." Her elucidation was all I needed to spur on. We discussed the manner of rectification on several other chapters now on hold for editing. Some of the developing chapters required no corrections whatsoever while others had either limited or very minor corrections in their structure. We were both pleased with the outcome of the rectifications.

These ensuing chapters both riveted J.B. and repulsed her at the same time. "It will be a most gripping expose of your life, but one that will certainly be a reckoning for those involved in such horrific deeds against minors now and in the future. Parents such as yours always seek to diminish their involvement when it comes to child abuse. The poor simply deny it while the rich hide their shame in institutions. Yours is not the only story of abuse. But it is far from what most children suffer. This, my dear, is what needs to be at the forefront of what is now considered blatant child abuse." She went on to clarify that the difference between the rich dealing with their unwanted children and the poor dealing with the same problems. The rich handed their children off to someone else to deal with while the poor were stuck with their offspring to cope in whatever way they could. Money makes a person hard in the heart but soft in the wallet. The poor, having no money, dealt with it as best as they knew how, learning from one generation to the next.

J.B. had then gone into a long-winded explanation of why child protective laws needed to be enacted into our system. "Verbal and physical abuse are generally triggered by emotional imbalances on the part of the parent committing the offense. This includes separating oneself from the child they feel ashamed of or the one they feel will prevent them from attaining their goals in life."

That made sense to me. My parents were considered pillars of the community and would never dare to admit they had a rebellious daughter who questioned everything. Or that they beat her for that rebellious streak. Many times, I had been beaten black am blue or until I bled, whichever came first.

J.B. continued "People suffer in different ways. Too often they never have the chance to distance themselves from the heavy invisible chains that bind them to cruel tormentors. And even more rare is the opportunity to declare in composition the depravity of some parents when it comes to their own children. This is where God sanctifies the gift of reaching out to others through the written word. This is where people, just like yourself, come in. people with a literary understanding that compels others to understand and perceive the pains of what parents are inhumanly capable of saying and doing to their children."

I asked J.B. if she felt my writing style was worthy of publication. Her reply caught me off guard. "It would be a pity if you did not submit it for publication. It is structurally sound, well-paced and has the potential for a movie script. This type of factual memories always lends to better movies. And I believe that this story, the way you are presenting it, can be beneficial to all involved in presenting it. whether that be by book publication or production through film. I hold your writing in high esteem. And I hope you have the courage to follow it through to the end." As usual I was not prepared for her response.

All too quickly I felt fear and doubt. I wanted to please this gentle editor, known only by her initials, but also wanted to prove to myself that I was capable of overcoming the worst nightmares of my life, my parents. "How do I know when to stop? There might still be memories left in me when the catastrophes are dealt with."

In her lilting tone J.B. quietly replied "As long as you live, there will always be memories, you have to decide which ones are valuable and significant to your story. The allure of the book is what is beneficial or advantageous to the reader. If you find the writing interesting, then so will your audience. Think about what you found appealing in books you have read in the past. That is where you begin your manuscript. Write as if you are speaking directly to each and every reader."

J.B. had a way of making me feel valued. Feel as if all my painful memories were for some spectacular reason. Somehow, I was meant to live out this dreadful existence. But do so in a rather sensible, meaningful way. These things were supposed to happen to me in my life. I had purpose now. Even if I did not understand that as J.B. had stated, I was at least willing to give it a try.

I had a few more questions for J.B. "What if they deny the contents of the book? I almost cried. In my mind I reasoned that if someone protested the accuracy of my memoir, that it would render the entire book invalid. I was soon to be educated on the fallacy of this notion.

"That will just mean they recognize themselves and as a result, will put credence to your book." I could tell she sympathized with my situation. "There will always be people around wo are eager to smear someone else with outright lies, innuendos, half-truths or twisted theories. I have certainly had my share of that to last me for the rest of my life.it gets to the point where you cannot even marry anyone out of love and respect without other people discrediting that marriage. You will hear "She married him for his money. He married her for her status. In most cases this is an unjustified speculation. If your truths do not pander to their scandalous implications, you must learn to excuse yourself from their existence and do what you know is right. Use your talent as a writer to forge on with what must be revealed." With J.B. clearly stating that, in her opinion, I had talent as a writer really bolstered my reserve. And I did want to rid myself of the memories that haunted me. So, this appeared to have merit as well as being a somewhat therapy for me. Not that I felt I needed any therapy. Silly me, I most definitely needed help, otherwise I would not have even bean to write.

I boldly ventured to ask a most personal question of this fine editor of whom I had grown to trust with my own secreted past. "J.B., how do you know so well about that particular inuendo? I am sorely trying to understand so that I too can prevail over such atrocities in my own life. That way I can put forth a more complete mini biography."

J.B. revealed she was just beginning to edit a book with a trusted colleague. "At the moment I am collaborating with Bill Moyers, of whom I am sure you know as a very respected television reporter and a prolific writer himself. Both of us are devoted to producing the best work in writing. When you are sure you have completed your manuscript to where your heart is at peace, then you will know you are done. Please continue towards wrapping up your story. After Bill and I are done with the current book at hand, I will contact you to see how your writing has fared." I did not get a direct answer to my question nor to the remarks I had made. In time I accepted her changing the subject as a means of not having to directly answer or if she preferred to avoid certain subjects.

As she explained the importance of punctuality and timing, I became nervous. I was nowhere near being finished. Not by a long shot. I began to wonder if my story would become obsolete by the time, I finished writing. I also wrote that J.B. had changed the subject in my notes. She did not say a word about my question. I was left to scan over my notations to calculate what lesson I was supposed to learn.

J.B. taught me that emotional writing was the best kind of writing for such a story as mine was. Feelings put into this kind of work garnished those same feelings in the reader. But did I really want to evoke those torturous reactions from my audience? The answer was apparent. Yes. Through those emotions that would be elicited from page after page, chapter by chapter, the individual could bring up pictures in their own minds of what that little girl suffered at the hands of her family at the age of four, seven and beyond into adulthood. Invaluable lessons learned that were heartbreaking at times but also dotted with small victories along life's path.

Throughout our conversations J.B. did not hold back on what she believed was too graphic in content. and also, on what was necessary for understanding the entire scene as it played out.

In simple terms J.B. would say "it is a very sad assumption that women are not supposed to work if they have children to raise and a household to attend to and manage. There are women across the world who hold various degrees but are virtually left to let their minds soften. Some are doctors, lawyers or scientists with brilliant minds. Working should be a choice, not a demand. Some are literary geniuses as you are. Or could be if you finish your manuscript. Complete use of one's faculties is an excellent way to convey a life affording one's scope." Beautiful words that I did not quite follow. Not then and not now.

Looking back in my memory, I could now see where living a nightmare might be useful to me as a tool in getting similar nightmares out in the open. Not just for me, but in suffering children as well, no matter what age those children were.

At this time, I would like to say that wherever exact wording is used, I have included it within the text. In some instances where the exact dialogue escapes me, I have inserted a summary of the conversation or have given it credence by way of opinion. This in no way changes the atmosphere of the conversations nor does it change the meaning of what both parties have stated.

An account of each phone call was immediately written down in a journal so as not to confuse myself as to what was stated, meant or learned. I read each account over and over until it was permanently engrained in my memory and came to me as easily as saying my own name. just as a person learns to recite the alphabet or count to ten, I knew each phone call that well. I would recite word for word to my husband what I had discussed with J.B. as each phone call came in. It is for this reason that I rely on exact wording wherever I can in presenting it to you, the reader. Hopefully you can get the feel or image of J.B. as you read each chapter.

Remember imagery is a powerful thing.

Chapter 4

It had been about a couple of months since my last phone call with JB. and I was at a part in my manuscript where my mother was pregnant with her sixth child. But also, at a point where death would be introduced into my life. In reality it was murder that I was trying to convey from a four-year-old girl's point of view.

It was an extremely difficult time because I had to relive the memory of it. The scene that had been plaguing me for the last several days was filled with bloody gore, intentional death and incredible sadness followed by bouts of anger and physical fights between my parents. I could not write a single word. J.B. had called this "Writer's block." Experiencing this block forced me to understand why some writers cannot complete portions of their books or were overwhelmed when faced with personal obstacles.

Broaching the subject, I found it hard to put the words together and felt quite embarrassed. But I had to ask J.B. how such a topic should be approached. She understood perfectly although my words were jumbled and almost incoherent. Her reply came before I finished my question. And I was relieved at her words and the sympathetic tone of her soft voice.

She began with "Murder is a hard, filthy word. My first husband was killed as I sat right next to him. Killing, ending or altering one's life is devastating. You must reach inside you to let others know and see what their actions have done not only to that person's loved ones, but also to the people who witness such a ruthless attack. When my husband was shot, I wanted them to see what they had killed. Not only another human being but a husband, father, uncle and a valued humanitarian. Let them see what they have done from a survivor's viewpoint" Her voice actually hardened as she related this horrendous part of her life. There was barely a hint of her gentle expression. And who could blame her? I was rooted to my seat as she relayed that living nightmare. And I am equally sure that she was reliving it just as I had to relive my childhood in all its wickedness.

There was so much that J.B. was telling me. Even more was what she was withholding. Curiosity got the best of me. I probed on, so sure I could get a fascinating view from a survivor's perspective. That survivor being J.B. From there I could best deliver my own storyline in a much more positive note. "I see you have firsthand knowledge or experience in this subject. I am so very sorry you went through that ordeal with your husband. Please accept my condolences. But I still need you to elaborate for me how you endured it and how you explained it to your family and others so they could fully understand the impact it had on you, and the consequences of what an act of thoughtless hate can cause." I needed to learn how to clearly express what I had seen and heard while I was a child. In a way I believe that it was essential for J.B. to speak of the atrocities in her life just as it was demanded of me to do likewise for the benefit of my manuscript.

A too long pause stirred thoughts of doom. Had I overstepped a boundary? Was she prepared to share details of her first husband's murder? I could not take back my words. They were out there, and I could only wait for an answer I might never get. I felt slightly faint.

Even a weave of nausea surfaced, and I had to swallow hard to hold back any physical spew. The silence was deafening while I waited for J.B. to speak. Regret filled me with shame for the question I had asked. Now it was too late to withdraw any part of it.

Then it happened. She began speaking softly and thoughtfully. "No one ever gets completely over it. First it wounds the heart, muddles the mind, then finally it scars the soul. No one is impervious. And if you are well known you had better have a strong backbone if you are to rise above conspiracy theorists, media, friend and even family. In Dallas, Texas our car was ambushed, and my husband was shot and killed as I sat next to him."

"How long ago did that happen? Was it just recently, like within the last few years?" her saddened tone brought tears to my eyes. I did not want to hear details anymore but was eager to learn from this at the same time. If J.B. could explain how to convey her tragedy, then I could likewise explain my baby brother's death. A deliberate death that left me scarred for the rest of my life.

"It was in 1963" she continued. A cold November day that was made colder by the fact that we were a convertible. It was suggested to us that a convertible be used on that particular day. My reaction, when it all happened, was to try to remove myself from being a target also. But I could not leave my dear husband to die alone. I could see that he was mortally wounded." She trailed off and I no longer wished to hear details. I berated myself for asking too many questions after the initial shock of the first inquiry. I should have known better than to keep asking about something that was none of my business.

Another long pause ensued while we both collected our thoughts and emotions. I finally broke the silence in an inadequate response. "How did you break the news to your family?" There it was again. I just could not help but be nosey. Inwardly I kept telling myself that it was not my concern. But I still could not keep my mouth shut. How would she respond to all my probing?

She answered more quickly this time. "I am not really sure how the news reached them. I only know I stayed by his side, his casket, as we flew back to the Washington D.C. area, and later to Virginia, where he is finally at peace." J.B. gathered her experience and shed light on it. This, in turn, helped me understand how to relay my own exposure to death. Her guidance in this matter was essential to me getting over this hurdle in my writing. I could now relinquish all my little girl anguish to pen and paper and leave it there. All the while images of J.B. and her husband floated just beyond my grasp. I had no idea what J.B. looked like, much less her husband's appearance. The date she gave me had gone right over my head. Without names or faces, the couple was virtually anonymous. And I believe she meant it to be that way.

She had told me that the writer was the most important part of the book. The one who imparted the story for the world to know. For the world to learn. For the world to change by way of reading a book. Yes, a single book could change a person's perspective. So. my manuscript could be that catalyst to enable someone to benefit from it and become stronger from it.

Once in a while I would look at the solitary correction, she originally made on my manuscript so many months before. It was in red ink. She had chuckled as she told me "Always carry a red ink pen with you. That way you will know if you wrote something of your own accord and writing. And not someone else's doing." Since then, I have always tried to carry a red ink pen in my purse. Most people carry black or blue ink pens. But very few tote red ink pens. It was a peculiar bit of advice, but to this day it is what I now try to do at all times. I do my own editing with it just as J.B. used her red ink pen to edit the first four chapters of my manuscript. I know when I do my own editing as compared to when someone else tries to correct me with any other color of ink. This bit of advice from J.B. has been a life saver at times.

How does someone describe a death when it is witnessed at such a young age as four years? Even after the conversation with J.B. I still struggled to maintain a balance between the horror of it all stemming from that tender age and to calmly writing about it as an adult. The feelings of a child were burdened with the weight of it while the adult me tried to coherently write the details without plunging into a deep depression. There had to be a midway to all the madness.

I clamored for answers that were hard for me to grasp. The uncertainty of how to write a manuscript in the firsts place was, in itself, more difficult than I expected. Now with the revelations of deliberate death in my family being exposed, made me feel as if my days were on borrowed sanity.

Hours and days were spent in a hazy fog just trying to find semblance in this chaotic venture that I had no business trying to accomplish. I began to experience the agony of failure as I tried endlessly to put pen to paper in a comprehensive manner. I was failing tremendously each time I tried to explain what I saw and heard on that fateful day in May 1956.

Now I was faced with the problematic job of writing about an incident that words could not explain. Listening to J.B. recall her own memory of death still did not fully qualify as an example for what I was trying to convey. J.B.'s experience involved a violent attack from an unknown entity. My issue with death was done in a quiet manner that involved a close family member. For all that J.B. told me, I could not use her advice or example this time. I was left in limbo for the first time after conversing with her.

For the rest of our conversations J.B. was a helpful and conscientious editor. And had it not been for her, I would never have had the opportunity nor the courage to continue with this literary project. For that I would forever be grateful.

Chapter 5

One day when I least expected it, J.B. called to ask about the details surrounding the death scene in my manuscript. She inquired about the length of time the entire ordeal took place. How long did it take me to clean up the blood that should have been reported? Where was my baby brother buried? Had I ever heard of the word exhumed? Aha! J.B. was now interested in much more detail. Now I would have the uneasy feeling of reliving that disgusting day when my baby brother ceased to exist at the hands of my mother.

J.B.'s tone was full of compassion which led me to trust her with my answer. She knew I could trust her as she trusted me with the revelation of her first husband's murder. We understood each other's pain and agony over the most heart wrenching details of our lives. Somewhere along the line she became more than just an editor. She was my mentor, guide, counselor and yes, even a long-distance friend.

The first time she addressed me as such came at a time when I was in utter confusion and despair over a memory of humiliation, public degradation, abuse and shame. I was on the verge of tears and was teetering over the most engrossing part when J.B. called. She knew the section of the chapter I would be writing on and guessed that I might need a slight encouraging word. That is true friendship when someone feels comfortable enough to reach out to you without any prompting. And that is exactly what J.B. was now doing. Her empathy was borne of her kind heart. Even though she had suffered in her own life, she was apt to be a guiding light to others. She was in all essence, a genuine caring human being. I fell short of being that kind of person.

She comforted me as tears fell, unwiped, from my eyes. Everything I wrote that day made me feel hollow. J.B. calmly assured me that it was only a memory. "It cannot touch you anymore unless you allow it to, my friend." Together we absorbed the moment. Then we both let it subside. She continued by letting me know that she had lost a child too. Albeit under different circumstances than what my baby brother went through. The scene I was describing was not by God's hand nor by accident. It was all my mother's doing, out of hatred because she had caught my father having an affair with her niece. My father had pretended to be giving my mother's niece a driving lesson but that is not what they were up to so late at night for almost two hours.

"You were only a child of four years. That blood that stained your clothing will forever be etched into your memory. I, on the other hand, left my bloody clothes on for everyone to see what their hatred and evil deeds had done. The consequences of self-preservation at the cost of someone else's life. My clothes were never washed, and the stain of their loathing remains to this day."

J.B. had given me another example of how dignity looks like when confronted with the atrocities of life. She had wept and grieved at the time of her husband's death but had overcome the burden with dignity and a newfound respect for life. All of this lesson was written down in my journal to study after our call ended. Every notation I wrote down after each call was studied and read over several times until I knew it by heart without having to refer to my notes afterwards. To this day I can recall our conversations with clarity and much more understanding.

As the writing slowed to a snail's pace, I began to notice that people on the streets and in the stores around town were beginning to stop and stare at me. Strangers would point at me, smile, and greet me. This would make me feel uncomfortable, as I did not know the majority of them. So often I would check my clothing to see if I had accidentally worn a shirt with a stain on it or worn it inside out. Then came the fateful day when I was coming out of the local drugstore. As I passed two women who were standing just outside the store's door, I smiled and greeted them. They smiled back and all was well. When I was leaving the store, they were still there. I got a few feet past them and quick as a whip one of the ladies grabbed my hair and clipped off a section.

In shock I screamed "My hair, my hair! You just cut off some of my hair. Why did you do that?" a clump of my hair was still dangling from the woman's hands as she gleefully exclaimed "I got it, I got it!"

That was it. If this was going to be the reaction of people in the small town of Selma, California, then what could a stranger in a big city do to me? I vowed to stop writing and just stay home where I knew I was safe. When my children came home from school, they chatted happily while enjoying the cupcakes I had baked for them earlier that morning. My son James noticed I was not in such a jovial mood. I was still in a state of sadness over what those two women had done to me. At this time in his life James was very sensitive to my moods.

I decided to be very honest with both of them. I explained to them what had occurred late that morning. My sons' faces turned ashen. Then sadness overcame them, and they admitted to telling their friends at school that I was writing a book about child abuse and witchcraft. It was the mothers of these school friends that had decided to just take a souvenir of their hometown author by whacking off a chunk of my hair. Now it all made sense. All the people who would stop and stare. The two women who were ready at hand with scissors, the lying-in wait until they could get what they wanted. Since I had not told anyone about what I was doing as far as writing, I did not put the strange incidents together with my manuscript.

I stopped writing. I began to seclude myself within the confinements of my home. There no one could stare, point or physically take parts off of me. I even avoided J.B. because I knew I would have to explain to her what had happened, and

I just did not want to go there. In my mind I deduced that if I did not think about it, it would go away.

I did not even bother to inform J.B. that I no longer wished to continue with my manuscript. Everything came to an abrupt stop. Sure enough J.B. took note of my silence. When I received a call from her, I knew I had to answer for my rude way of ending my contact with her. And, of course, J.B. was not going to spend time on pleasantries. She came right to the point after the initial hellos.

"M.S. I was wondering how your work was going. I call it work because I know it is just as difficult to relive and write down specific memories that may haunt your life." Her words were somewhat of a blur. "And do not ever forget that this is actual work. Just as surely as if you were to clock in at a commercial job. Now tell me how much product you have accomplished since the last time we talked."

Here it was. The time had arrived when I had to assess my fears. I knew she would tell me that I had to overcome the stigma of being recognized whenever I stepped out of my front door. I had to confess to J.B. that I was not ready to accept that kind of recognition. I tried explaining to her that that I just did not have it in me to continue with the shame, the blot, the disgrace of having the family background that would eventually reveal my identity. The blemish this would leave was not what I had anticipated. I wanted to feel pride in my work. I wanted what I had never had in my life before. High self-esteem. If I wrote about this for very much longer, I would feel as if I would adversely brand my family for the rest of their lives. That was not a gamble I was ready to take. I had hoped J.B. could understand that. Maybe I had banked on something that was out of character for her. In either case, she refused to let me back down from the work that she believed in.

In her ever-calming voice J.B. once again had to guide me over this mountain of trepidation. How she must be tiring of having to do so just to get what she believed was a great story worthy of publication. "The agitation you feel now" she began, "will diminish in time. No literary work that has been successful has been without its doubts, misgivings or other fears that have caused blocked writing. This, I believe, is what you are experiencing. I am certain of it." How could she say something like that to me in such a calm way? Did she not understand dhow traumatic that scene was with those two women? For the first time I had doubts about J.B.'s involvement in this venture. She bypassed the fear within me and proceeded to filter it all out with the simple word of agitation.

"Agitation? This seems like way more than mere agitation." I coolly replied. "When a person feels like they have the right to cut off a lock of another person's hair, what will stop them from doing harm to that person? Intentional or not. I cannot risk that. I have a family to think about."

Again, J.B. knew exactly what I was referring to. "Let me tell you something about fame. The more fame you have, the more risks you have each time you leave your home. Think about the president's wife. Any president. There is a mother, a First Lady, who has children to think about. A home to maintain. Yet, she has to leave her home and take risks because someone may either love or hate her or her husband a bit too much. Are you taking any more of a risk than a woman who is known around the world? There is always something, a chance that you might encounter some danger outside your home. Whether or not you are well known that risk is there. There is also always the possibility that you could make a change in this world, in your life, if you took that step. A step that could save lives, not just yours, but others like you." J.B. really knew how to make a person feel guilty by using simple logic.

Now I felt ashamed for not thinking of others. My selfish need to protect myself and not worry about others in this same situation came to light and J.B. called me on it. She did not let up on it when I failed to answer immediately. "Believe me when I say I know precisely how you feel and what your concerns are."

Stunned into silence when J.B. first called, I now knew I had to explain my alarm in proceeding with this manuscript. After stumbling over my words, I eventually mumbled out the events in front of the drug store. Without regard to the time, it took to convey my encounter with the two women in town, I thoroughly went from the time I left my house, the attack by one of the women, until I returned home. I had felt exhausted, humiliated, helpless, all the negative things I did not want to relive.

"How dare they just take a physical part of me? I cannot go out my front door comfortably if I expect to be attacked." The plea for understanding burst forth in the tone of my voice as I began to shrill with desperation. "I am scared." I finally spat out. "I do not now or ever will have your reserve, J.B., your confidence or security of self. I prefer to listen, or to read someone else's clever writings. Books that interest me are the non-fiction stories with true literary meaning." Being one with that caliber of authors is not the real me. And I tried to make her see that I could not compete in that category of esteemed writers.

Now this previously soft-spoken editor became a source of strength as she raised her voice only slightly, though enough for me to catch on that she meant business. I pictured a lioness in my mind as she spoke in more deliberate enunciation than I had ever heard coming from her in any of our conversations. It chilled me to think about what she might say using that tone of voice.

"And what do you suppose your life story is? Definitely not a children's book. These pages you are writing constitute decades of torture, abuse, not only as a child but well into adulthood. The progression of physical contact was soon supplemented with mental and emotional abuse. What I am trying to make you understand is that you were too young to realize that there was more than the incest going on at the hands of your father. And both of your parents tried to rid themselves of their own guilt by blaming you. They groomed you to be silent. To not be seen or recognized by anyone. Now you are being faced with the challenge of recognition." Boom! J.B. had the wisdom of a counselor, as well as an editor.

Her resolve to get things completed through counseling made me suspect that she had, at some point in her life, been through counseling herself, although she did not admit to that. But I was grateful for her patience with me whenever I struggled to finish this dreary project that I now felt locked into. I wondered what I had gotten myself into. I knew it would be the last time I would ever write a manuscript.

I was also afraid that I might have ruined the budding friendship that we had established from a mutual understanding of life's atrocities. I felt chained to this manuscript and did not realize the benefits it could bring at this time.

Chapter 6

The dawning of a new era had turned its wheels. Strength and determination revved up from somewhere deep in my soul. It was true. J.B. had struck a nerve that could not be denied. My parents were devious in their plans to destroy me. They talked me down to friends and relatives alike. They knew they would be believed because of their money, donations to the Catholic church and school systems. And amongst the relatives, they looked at my parents as being successful and with hidden money. This made it easy for my parents to deceive people about their fake friendships and about my own status in the family.

My parents' hatred of me started early in my life and continued throughout my life. I was berated in front of family and friends so that they could prove haw horrible a person I was. Ans, of course since I was silenced, I did not even have the chance to set things clear with the relatives. But now I had the tenacity to lift the veil of secrecy. Whether or not I would be accepted as part of the family again is of no concern to me. I lived my life without familial ties, and I did not miss the squabbling and back biting that comes with it.

"I am sure they will deny everything." I slowly stated. "But they know I am telling the truth. But they will not be able to deny the physical scars on my body."

J.B. then had an idea. "Take pictures of all the scars you have, if they can be shown. They are verification of what you say in your manuscript." This is where I drew the line. Some of those injuries marred my body and were easily recognizable as being a part of me. Anonymity would vanish with the first picture. Anonymity is what I craved for, but I began to understand that being a writer means exposing yourself as well as the people you write about. It was either a winning bet or a losing bet. Deep down inside I knew it did not really matter to me. According to my mother the relatives had a lot to be ashamed of and with a lot of reason to keep their lives hidden from the truth. If their pasts were just as devious as Momma had described, I had no reason to accept them into my life anyway.

A turbulent past has a way of rearing its ugly head when you least expect it. As I glanced over the physical scars left by a mother who was supposed to protect me, I began to consider that maybe I had actually done something to deserve such a fate. J.B. had said that a child is never at fault in these matters. But what if she had erred in her judgment? Maybe somewhere along my life I had provoked my parents into being cruel and unjust in their way of thinking. Had I been responsible for my parents going insane? It had never occurred to me that parents could insane. I thought parents were supposed to know everything and that they could make sound judgments in the lives of their children. I could only hope to not be as cruel to my own children as my parents were to me.

It was almost time for my children to come home from school. It was then that I realized that I did not know step one of how to be a proper parent. Anxiety over how much damage I had already caused them made teardrops fall gently down my cheeks. I would be mistaken if I had felt that I knew how to raise them. I would be responsible for whom they would eventually become as adults. Would they understand that I was growing up with them and not before them? And that we were learning together on how an adult should be portrayed in public as well as in private? The only thing I knew for sure was that my babies were intelligent and had a part of me in them. In that, they could face the world with a strong conviction that they could accomplish anything.

Within a few weeks J.B. was calling yet again to inquire about the progress of the manuscript. She understood the difficulty I was experiencing. Giving moral support and sound advice were her chief principles. Her priority was to establish trusting rapport with her prospective author and her colleagues. So far, she had built a trusting relationship with me on this collaboration. She began attentively, not knowing what to expect from me, but still willing to work with my unbalanced writing routine.

"M.S. I am calling in regard to your last two chapters. How often did your mother choke you into unconsciousness? I understand that you were quite young when it began and your guess as to the number of times can only be an approximation. But if you could assert yourself as closely as possible to the times, ages of when you were throttled, what triggered their onslaught of abuse and where it happened, it would help in clarifying the situations. And, again, pictures are evidence of truth. The longer you wait, the ravages of time on your skin can forever erase or diminish your evidence. And it is those scars that no one can deny."

J.B. wanted me to elaborate on the details of my physical scars. This was still foreign to me as far as the manuscript was concerned. I saw no value in them, so I just said I would think about it. I knew all the while that I did not want to pursue the picture aspect of the book. Anyone who has physical scars knows that if they are visible at a glance, they can identify who the person is. If I were to post pictures in this book, I could be more readily identifiable.

Once more J.B. pinned me down as to what my future would entail. Wrinkles, sagging skin and even age spots could diffuse my proof. The manifestation of physical scars indicated that what I stated was pure fact. Exhibiting my wounds corroborated my trauma as an undeniable documentation. My suffering would be substantiated so that no one could ever deny what occurred in my daily life. She kept on echoing her rhetoric about how pictures could be substantial in letting the reader actually see what was being described in certain scenes. J.B. kept droning on until my head was pounding with the pain of a migraine coming on. My only relief was in continuing to confide in her about my childhood nightmares.

Engulfed by the odd story that was unfolding before her eyes, J.B. had become more sympathetic to my plight. "There are people in foreign lands who hold only their children as valuable assets as compared to owning mass acreage of land or large homes. The imagined entitlement of wealthy parents in America to infringe upon one of their own children is an odious thought. Bringing in the other family members as a way to wield their strength of authority is just downright inhuman. I am sincerely astonished that they did not lock you up somewhere other than a dark closet. For instance, a sanitarium. I know of such a family where the parents did not want their rebellious daughter to be known of low degree because of her love of freedom. So, the father conspired with his two elder sons to eliminate her much too carefree manner by institutionalizing her and later convincing the staff doctors to perform an unnecessary lobotomy on this young girl. And because she was admitted by her wealthy prominent father, no questions were asked as to why they wanted it performed. They were just paid to do a specific job and to keep it confidential."

No questions asked in an unnecessary surgery? What kind of doctor would even cater to such a request? It was at this time that I learned that money is the root of all evil, but that money makes all the difference in the world where politics and science are concerned. There is no room for integrity and honesty when an abundance of money is introduced into the equation.

Wow! J.B. did know about hardships in life that go unregistered within the confines of familial circumstances. She could prove all that she was revealing but stopped short of actually naming any one particular family. Although she did mention that they were a very wealthy and prominent family known for accumulating their wealth and status partly through the stock market and alcohol. But were also known through politics where the sons were most prominent.

J.B. had a colorful, yet mysterious way of relaying her examples. Her view on wealth was that it changed a lot of people who would otherwise be humble and loving sorts. She knew how to reveal secrets without imparting too many intimate details. That is what she was teaching me. How to reveal what I wanted my audience to know. And what I wanted them to imagine what they knew. But all within the guidelines of honesty. Everything had to be the truth if this little biography of an unknown writer was to be believed. I had to somehow find a way to engage the reader in page after page of truth. Changing names to protect the innocent would also include protecting the guilty. But it would still contain provable facts. Altering the names of a city or town would not hinder the outcome of reality. Only if I felt comfortable enough to elaborate on certain verity would I put it down and the same thing with actual or exact names.

I pondered the thought of renaming my siblings and parents. It was too tempting. What a devilish little tidbit of advice from J.B. I jotted down names that I most detested and that fit their personalities. This was the best time I had in writing the story that was otherwise bleak and tormenting for me. I laughed so hard at the names I was giving to each one of them. Laugh, laugh, laugh. I did so enjoy this trek of my story. So, I took my time renaming my siblings. Not much could be done about my parents. They would remain Momma and Daddy for now. I did not care enough to give them an identity.

J.B.'s words resurfaced every now and then. She had refused to tell me what names she abhorred. "This is your story, M.B. You know better than anyone what their personalities are and what names suit them the best for this particular storyline. How delicious, though, to be able to express your thoughts and feelings in the form of renaming them and still remaining anonymous to a certain extent."

We paused and chuckled, then J.B. proceeded with a caution. "Do not allow anagrams of their names to come into focus. One of them might take notice and file suit against you for exposing their dark dirty secrets." "One" of them? We burst out in full blown laughter. She clarified "I would never infer that any members of your family are slow witted or not intelligent. But as the tale goes, being sly or devious takes almost as much intelligence as a more astute person."

By now J.B. had me convinced that I was one of the astute people. The ones who could giggle at an inner joke. I was amused at J.B.'s way of verbalizing her illustrations. Our camaraderie remained intact in spite of my refusal to write for a brief moment in time.

How I wanted to write in the same manner in which J.B. spoke. Her cultured phrases enunciated in such delicate wording. Somehow, I sensed, that probably would take half a lifetime for me to even begin to accomplish. But something I would strive for, nonetheless. I would play devil's advocate in releasing a tell all story of what happens in households and in families that people never suspect of wrongdoings. For that matter the shock of my revelations may not even be accepted as truth. All my relatives had to do was believe every word that spewed out of my parents and siblings. That is how convincing my family could be. It did not matter if I had physical proof or witnesses to establish my honesty in the manuscript. If my family refused to accept being exposed, then everyone associated with them would not believe it either.

J.B. continued. "From all the examples, proof, physical scars and other facts, all it would take is one denial from any person depicted in your script, to make the reader fall into a state of confusion because that is all they have ever known. But why go through even a single denial if they truly believe it is not them being exposed? In that sense, they are exposing themselves, not by your hand. If you are writing a book about strangers, then it will not affect their egos."

J.B. made more and more sense each time she advised me on how to reveal specific incidents without readily opening up actual identities. She guided me on how to optimize my story while keeping anonymity for victims and aggressors alike. Decades of lies, secrets, backstabbing, abuses and witchcraft were not only prevalent in my family but in others as well. Deep rooted friendships were not real after all, they only appeared to be. But to lay bare how my family genuinely thought of them was going to be a bit toilsome to disclose.

I explained to J.B. that many people considered that their bonds with my family to be close knit. So many never considered that their dear friends were only using them. They never realized that there was some evil lurking behind smiling faces.

This in itself proved that my family would seek out simple minded people in which they could control or easily convince of anything. To this day I knew that they still were fooling people into believing anything they said. In a recent meeting right before I began writing my manuscript, I was told I was at fault for all my problems, as they had heard from my siblings and parents that I just could not follow direction from them. Words such as stupid, dumb, bible thumping, and such descriptions would cause laughter and conviction in those who paid attention to their lies and innuendos.

Chapter 7

I found my situation was not unique in the least bit. J.B. volunteered that she had encountered people who seemed to be authentic with their friendships, only to discover that that was not the case. "It does not matter if you have become acquainted with someone for a few weeks or a few decades. There will come a time when their other face will be revealed, and it will up to that person to either accept the facts or to go on living the lie with which they have become accustomed to. Some people actually prefer the lie."

I know this to be true. My eldest sister has these types of association with people. From her high school years and even into adulthood. Placidity was more important than facts. She is highly allergic to the truth as is my other sister who hides her lesbianism from anyone who might question her authority on family values. Neither one knows the true value of familial ties.

To further accentuate the absurdity of blind loyalty, J.B. mentioned that it could be a way to come to a conclusive end. "You will find yourself at a crossroads when this story unveils the truth, and you lose some respect from those continue to follow your family. But in the long run you will be well respected by people who understand that the truth is eminent power."

I did not want J.B. to know that I had no interest in power of any kind. Except the power of an honest reveal of abuses suffered by a little girl too young for those atrocities. I sympathized with children who were considered the black sheep of their families. I saw firsthand what too much power can do to someone's ego. I did not want to fall prey to that same sickness that engulfed my parents and siblings. I did not want to be responsible for lowering another person's self-worth.

Conversations with J.B. were the highlights of my days. The wisdom she imparted was invaluable and I trusted her advice more and more with each phone call. I still had not met her after all these months. Not only did I not have the funds to travel all the way to New York, but my manuscript was only half completed. I could tell

J.B. was beginning to be impatient with me, but at the same time giving me the space and time I needed to get it done right. She was not about to waste her time on a project that would, in the end, not be a publishable piece of literary work.

Her words became more urgent. "I need to view your latest chapters if this is going to be a finishes manuscript. This is not a fictional piece of literary work where you must research for the next character, scene or correct dialogue. It is already within you. You need only to relax your emotions and let the memories flow. You can relax, can't you?" she ended sarcastically. "Just do whatever eases your mind. You mentioned housework, baking, artwork and gardening. While performing your chores or pleasures, think about what has happened in your life that first prompted you to start a journal about your life. Allow the memories to speak for themselves without any deliberate provocation on your conscious part. Once you give way to both the happy and the sad moments, simply pick up your pen and continue writing as the scenes flash before your eyes."

She had to have known that as a first-time writer, that would be an impossibility for me. Especially because of the content of material I was writing about. Why would she push me so hard on a subject that I am sure she herself would find difficult to complete? With all these thoughts racing in my head I still could not bring myself to question her educated knowledge and experience in the literary world of publishing. I guess you could say that had to do this alone on my end of the stick.

I was alone for seven hours a day, five days a week. My household chores and gardening finishes, I began a routine of sipping a cup of cinnamon tea with pen and paper at hand. Sure enough, the pages began to fill up faster than I could have ever imagined. Within a couple of months, I was ready to send J.B. more chapters for review. She was not disappointed. In fact, her praises for the completed work were overwhelming, but were genuinely expressed. I felt elated. My work was at long last verified to be to be written as cohesively as any actual published author.

And J.B. let me know she was pleasantly surprised to read the latest chapters. "I can see that little four-year-old girl.

What I mean is that I can envision the circumstances in which she was forced to accept as her life swirled in between bouts of quiet anger that she surely must have felt as she endured the consequences of her parents' wrath. I could not put down the manuscript once I started reading it." That is what I was hoping against hope for. That the reader cannot put the book down once they start reading. I had read books like that. The author had written their story so well that I just had to find out what was going to happen next.

Her words, like in other conversations, were emblazoned in my heart. I would never forget her words. Her confidence spilled over, and she made a bold prediction as far as my literary skills were concerned. "I predict that this story will be made into a great movie if it falls into the right hands. And this will not be your only story. I feel there are many truths to be unveiled in their own proper times.

Given the proper opportunities, you will find other hidden memories come to light and you will certainly be just as successful with them as I know this one will be." I was breathless. More books? I could not even finish this project, much less others.

Secretly I never imagined what an ending would look like for my book. Nor could I look beyond that to any further books or notes that centered around my life. I did not title my manuscript. The title came from my husband after he awoke from a dream where he saw me in a bookstore surrounded by people wanting my autograph for a book with the title 'Of Demons Past'. I liked the title but was unsure how

J.B. would react to it.

When I confided to J.B. about the title, she gave her utmost approval. "That sums it up perfectly. Go with that one." I thought I detected a very slight chuckle. "Those demons are definitely in your past where they belong and there they will stay." She approved and now I had a permanent title for my manuscript.

Simplicity in speech. J.B. knew full well how to get her point across. Especially with her soft-spoken manner that evoked confidence not only in herself, but to whomever she was speaking to. I know for sure it worked on me. And worked so well that I no longer cried during the memory floods.

After housecleaning, baking, gardening, and getting prepared for dinner, my time was fully invested in writing my biography. I had no qualms about highlighting the many abuses and lies that my family came up with. Whether or not anyone accepted them as fact was dependent on their own upbringing and beliefs. They were not my concern. To this day there are still some who believe every single word that my family utters. I pity them. But, in their convictions that they truly were friends then and now, that their friends were honest then and now, is what keeps their sanity afloat.

A woman who believes she was a friend, even to this day, asked me a question that she was not prepared to honestly hear the answer to. "How is your family doing?"

I answered her by simply saying "I don't know. I have not spoken to them in decades."

Taken aback, in anger she said "I don't want to hear that. The answer is 'they're doing fine.'" After this we never spoke again. Her fantasy world is her salvation, and she is entitled to it. She thought she was my eldest sister's best friend. I could not take that away from her. Thus, I have often allowed people their fantasies about what life in reality is, and life in imagination is to them. I learned a valuable lesson that day.

As our phone calls progressed J.B. hinted that a collaboration with her colleague might be coming to a fruitful end. She would then be able to extend more of her helping hand in my manuscript. She was intrigued by the fact that I had endured not only the severe beatings but the extreme brutality in the mental and emotional incidents. I could not argue with her on that. She urged me to find some happy moments in my life to intersperse around the abuses.

I supposed that I could have filtered some happy moments throughout my life and that is what kept me sane and alert. But I was still damaged goods as I was made to be painstakingly aware of when I became a parent myself. J.B. had said "If you have no guidance, no decent example, no family support, then yes, you are bound to make mistakes. Even if you think you know better, you may still err on that side of parenting. Your children may even resent you. But if they learn from it, then it was worth a hundred mistakes. In the end, it is up to them to understand and realize why you did not make good sound judgment calls as other parents do. And if they are anything like you, their intelligence will aid them in making loving and forgiving decisions."

J.B. was on target. I had already made many mistakes in raising my children. And I knew I would continue to make errors of judgement, even if I knew better. I hated knowing that I had hurt my children in some way. Their trust in me was deep. So, their resentment would be even deeper.

J.B. caught my solemness. "Do not regret for one minute what you have taught your children. Right or wrong, there is a lesson for them in it all. If they can comprehend the facts of your life, they will eventually come to grips with it."

J.B. spoke as if she had lived through some of my misery just by reading about it. I felt sadness well up inside me. She was so kind and gentle to have gone through any type of heartache. And now she was willing to carry mine. Such a burden that I did not even want to carry it myself. But she was willing to do just that.

Well, it was time to hang up the phone again. J.B.'s final words seemed more like a precaution. "Remember that you are not infallible. Just as your parents made mistakes, you are also apt to make errors in judgment while raising your children. But unlike your parents, I am sure you will invoke the spirit of success in your own children. How can they not succeed? They are a part of you. Your temperament, your vices may naturally become their vices. They may not acknowledge that, but you will recognize yourself in how they react to certain situations. And, my friend, we all have vices. Your parents have them and some of them may have overlayed onto you and the way you see things. Inadvertently, you will pass them onto your children. Only time will tell. Through your story and history this will e revealed. Those with higher cognitive abilities in the field of psychiatry and psychology will definitely be able to strain through the pages for a deeper more clinical evaluation of this life story. From a literary standpoint it will awaken peoples' perspectives on the hidden secrets of society."

J.B. was long winded today. Her sense of urgency to spur me on was eident and I did not, could not, fathom as to why. However, I am an inquisitive soul. "J.B., are you alright? Is there something you are deliberately not telling me? I may be reading more into your words, but I feel as if you are holding back on something. Is it something I have said or done? Please clarify what the problem is."

Clarification did not come forth easily from J.B. where her private life was concerned. Destined to be selective about anything in her past that could identify her, J.B. calmly stated "There has been more than enough from our conversations to let you know what I have been through. Whereas my childhood may not be as traumatic as yours has been, my adult life has had its own disquieting and traumatic moments." She knew when to stop short of divulging too much information. In doing so she taught me how to reveal my past without pouring out every sordid detail. Too much documentation clouded the pertinent facts. Details on certain incidents, yes.

Overwording, no. this not only highlighted the particulars of the storyline, but it did so in a concrete fashion.

J.B. clarified her statements. "Get that portrayal out and go to the next scene before the audience gets bored with too much redundancy. Not that life or story or manner of writing is redundant." J.B. quickly added. "But a few examples within each decade is enough to allow the reader to grasp the scenario of what is happening, how it manifested, and when it occurred, as far as age sequence." Now she was instructing me on how to write in an orderly technique. I could not ask for a better, more caring editor as

J.B. was. With her knowledge of literary works, and the fact that she said she had published works of her own, along with her sister, I was secure in her advice. It occurred to me that she never really told me what the title of her book was. And I was too self-absorbed in my own work that I never gave it a second thought. But J.B. was an editor. She knew her job quite well. And she was giving me the chance to succeed for the first time in my life.

It was at this point that I realized that people come into your life to make it complete, concise, and to allow you the freedom to explore your own world on your own terms. Some of these people, like J.B., are only there for a specific purpose and then they are gone, reaching for that next assignment. I was grateful for J.B.

Chapter 8

By following J.B.'s instruction, I moved along in my composition much more smoothly than before all her advice came along. The drudgery of inexperience was replaced by sound reasoning. This was the moment that I felt experience was speaking to me through the telephone wires. Experience. The elixir of success was J.B.'s experience which she shared with me in an unselfish coming together of the minds. Hopefully I could learn to have cultured manners like hers in due time. In the meantime, I lived on borrowed kindness and class from her. She had said imagery was a powerful thing. Well, I imagined I could be kind and giving.

J.B. explained her part in the handling of my work. "My publications have been nonfictional too. But they have been in collaboration with my sister. We documented our travels together as young women. That was a delightful sort of reading. Nonfiction, but in a whimsical balance to other nonfiction or biographical volumes. Short biographies are the best as they get right to the meat of the narration. No ruffly side views." Right to the meat of the story is what I was having problems with. There was too much meat to contend with and I was butchering what was there.

I was not proficient enough in the literary aspect to put together an entire book. The meat of it was almost unbearable. The best I thought I could do was maybe a side dish to go along with the meat of a manuscript. I tried to avoid talking about it at this time, so I took a cue from J.B. when she did not care to discuss something. I changed the subject.

I wanted to hear more about her travels. "Where did you and your sister travel to?" maybe one day I could visit distant lands like the ones J.B. exalted about. She was in a state of extreme happiness as she exclaimed it was an exciting trip to Europe, where they met noblemen, millionaires, and other people with exciting lives. She mentioned that if I found something exciting in my life, then I should include it in the storyline. My problem was that I did not find my life exciting. Only tragic.

"Make your autobiography interesting. Add a few references of joy and happiness, if you can recall any. Intersperse them within the gloom of your otherwise drama and fears. Too much of a bad thing does not make for a good reading. Adults, at times need a break from pure misery. From the hardships of reality. We all crave an intervention from all the sordidness that binds us in our daily lives."

Conversations with J.B. had immensely guided me in how to display my childhood. Although I did not remember a single moment before the age of four, I am certain it was not as deliberately or cruelly savage as before that age. At least I assume it was a more normal life. Oddly enough my own children have memories that they can recall from the age of two or three. How splendid that must be. I would love to have that kind of recall to see if I had ever experienced a normal childhood at any time. Instead, I had to rely on the memories of my older siblings to fill in the gaps.

My eldest sister would later tell me that my father did not want to bring me home from the hospital after I was born. He wanted to abandon me. My mother had to think twice on whether or not she wanted me at all. This bit of information outright saddened J.B. She attempted to console me.

"Maybe deep within their hearts they knew that you would be the keeper of their sins. How utterly unstable that probably made them. You are still here, still alive for some reason. Do not let that reason be wasted. Instead, be the salvation in spite of it." J.B. forced me to acknowledge the fact that if anyone were to salvage anything memorable from not only my childhood but from my life up to now, it would have to be me.

Sometimes J.B. was a wee bit confusing, but I did not want her to think of me as dimwitted. So, I said I understood when she asked if I had comprehended what she was saying. I would spend hours contemplating her more educated way of speech. I had to decipher some of it, but I finally was able to comprehend the gist of what she was saying to me.

What I clearly understood were the praises she heaped upon my work. There were, however, some accolades that I loved to hear her testify to on my behalf. For example, the time I had said I wished or longed to write in a more sophisticated and educated expression of language. She smoothly crooned in a sing song tone "But, my friend, you have no idea how excellent your grasp of the language is. It is an incredible display of how a soul truly speaks of its abuses and healings. And what you cannot find in your soul, look in a dictionary." I laughed at that last remark without thinking of whether or not I had hurt her feelings when she was just trying to help me out on this manuscript. But I was pleasantly amused at her way of saying it.

Aha! J.B.'s sense of humor took over our conversation and we both relaxed for a few moments before venturing back to the task at hand. But not before J.B. told of one of the many times her first husband often played on the floor in his office with their children.

"I even have pictures to prove it. There he was on his hands and knees smiling while his back was in immense pain. I later chided him that he had no excuse for not enjoying football games with his family, swimming parties, golfing or other activities he and his brothers loved to be sport to."

We both laughed at her special memories because they were the good times that she lived out among the sad incidents of her own life. She had said I also held joyous moments in my life that were crucial to my own history. A history put into a narrative with both good and evil. This made my memories more bearable. More normal. More worth writing about. I thanked J.B. many times over for her imprint on my life. Where would I have stopped writing had it not been for her encouraging words, her wisdom, her own literary talent?

Modesty was prevalent as she hesitantly replied in her usual soft voice. "No, I believe you would have had the courage and ability to produce this work sooner or later. With or without me. Let your confidence lead you. And you do have confidence, otherwise you would never have written the first line. Or even the first word for that matter."

I vehemently disagreed with her on that. I had no way of knowing that she was correct. I would have more memories to write about. More adventures to digest and bring forth so I could share with the world. It was the sharing with the world that had first made me hesitant about writing. But as I grew bolder within my heart and mind, the clearer the future looked to me.

I knew I could trust J.B.'s intuition. She had consistently been accurate throughout all her assumptions and understanding of my childhood experiences. J.B. was also accurate about how my adult life was manifesting because of each and every episode. "The impact of it all has led you to where you are able to confront it peacefully in your heart. Going forth from here on out to its conclusion is just a matter of will, determination, and the knowing that this is the only way to claim justification for your many hardships. Do not succumb to its lethal power over you. Its power has run its course. You have stripped that strength from them and now you have potential to set the record straight with facts. Provable facts."

How simple J.B. made it seem. The probability was indeed there. What J.B. did not quite comprehend was that I had been taught at an early age to accept my dire consequences and to not fight back. No matter what was said and done to me or about me. This was the obstacle that I knew without a doubt that I had to prevail over if I was to succeed at anything. Even anything beyond this manuscript. But by the same token I understood that I could not do it alone. There were still to come the days when I curled up on my bed in a fetal position listening to the sobs echo in my throat and the pounding in my head because of the memories that haunted my lonely days.

I would write down the memories as if someone else was dictating to me about another person's life. But for the most part I held my own and was able to write as if I had been doing manuscripts my entire life. Yet, what should have been hurdles to cross, it was more reminiscent of mountains to cross. No, I knew full well that this journey would definitely need a compassionate soul to hold my hand and assure me that I was doing this for all the right reasons. And the first reason was to clear my soul of the barbarity in my childhood. Appalling as it was, it was the fodder of which my manuscript was based on.

My husband's jobs kept him away in ever increasing hours and days. My children were too young to be burdened with all the trauma that was unfolding and revealing the insanity of their grandparents and other family members. No, that was not for them to carry. I may not have been the best mother, nor the best example of parenthood for them. But I dearly loved my children and had no idea how to express that to them. Not then, not now.

I asked J.B. if I should include them in the manuscript. She was honest, as always, in her opinion. "They were not a part of your past. Nor have they harmed you in any way now in your present life. To place them in an area where they do not belong is not only unfair to them but will endanger the accuracy of events. In my opinion they should be left out of this book. They can later be included in their own stories depending on how they turn out as adults." J.B. was straight forward in her opinion. Not only did she not hesitate to answer my question, but she did not in any way try to avoid it.

Of course, I already suspected what her answer would be but needed, no, craved her validation. If she could corroborate my own concept or opinion on the matter, then I knew for sure that I had learned from our many conversations and her sage advice. I was finally learning how to listen to someone else's advice without feeling offended or like they were attacking me.

J.B. gave examples along the way to make me feel comfortable in her abilities as an editor, established author, and as an empathetic human being. She related facts about firsthand knowledge of people she encountered that would bring tears to my eyes or leave me in shocked disbelief. Granted they were not all about death, as in the case of her husband, but of the barbaric savagery that she had witnessed in others who had come and gone throughout her life. If such a delicate heart could withstand that enormity of nefariousness, then I could learn to do likewise.

J.B. began her confidence speech. "You are worthy of expelling this darkness from your soul. It is the only key to survival. I have been in your situation before. And not just once. You may face many critics by the time this chapter in your life is completed. And even worse, questions and doubts by the time enough people have read your book. But always keep your head up. Do not look back with regret. Just let truth lead your way."

J.B. could sometimes sound philosophical. That sugary voice could turn the tide when she felt the need to get to the bare truth. "Now, no more delays. Get that work done now! And make sure it is done properly." And there it was. The dragon in her came out when it was necessary to get things moving along.

Okay then...okay! By now I was approximately three fourths of the way done. Revisions were a constant. I had to pull up scenes and conversations to get accuracy and exact wording if it was even possible. J.B. had told me "If the wording does not come, then make the scene with such clarity that it will convey the wording without actual dialogue."

This, I found, to be my saving grace. For how was I to repeat the language uttered to me by someone when I was only four years old? Or at the age of seven? Even if I could not distinguish their words verbatim, the acts my parents carried out were crystal clear. Remembering all that would have to do. And remember I sadly did.

Coming to grips with this realization made it possible for me to continue with my work. Albeit it was moving along too slowly for J.B.'s liking but it was going in the right direction. It was going in my direction at my pace for the first time. And I had no regrets about the rhythm of the writing.

I informed J.B. that I could write at my own pace as long as she allowed me to. She agreed to back off from calling for a while. A short while. Her instincts told her I may need her guidance with each memory stumbling block. And she was correct. I needed guidance but nonetheless tried to complete the manuscript on my own without running to J.B. at my every whim.

Chapter 9

Learning from J.B. gave me a sense of liberation from the chains of evil bondage. Encouragement is what I needed almost on a daily basis. This I knew for sure. And J.B. was just a call away. Convenience without worry or stress. She was more readily available to me than my husband with his two full time jobs. I had no friends that I could trust enough to confide in. so J.B. became my only ally. The keeper of the skeletons in my closet. She knew this and never once did she betray that confidence. The impact of her in my life was built on trust. So, when she called me "friend" I knew instinctively that it was genuine camaraderie.

J.B. had once described our relationship as "esprit de corps." Which is French for fellowship and common loyalty. She spoke French as well as other languages, as I found out along the way. J.B. was well versed in different dialects. Her vernacular was incredible. And her perceptive insight was right on target. One conversation went like this:

J.B.: "Comment allez-vous, mon ami?"
(How are you, my friend?)

Me: "tres bien merci, et vous?"
(Very well thank you, and you?)

J.B.: "Ca ne pourrait pas etre mieux."
(It couldn't be better.)

It was a joy to hear her speak in French. And it brought a lightness of heart to the subject at hand. By now my manuscript was nearly completed. But I had to relate to J.B. the tragic news that my mother- in-law had passed away. I would not be writing for a few weeks while my family mourned her death. Whether or not I had flashbacks or memories come through, I would respect my husband's mother and not work during this time of grief. My husband finally took time off from his jobs.

"I have no idea exactly how long it will be before I pick up my pen again. My mother-in-law was more like a mother to me than my own biological mother ever was. The kind of mother I wished for while growing up. It will take me a long while to get over this grief in my heart."

"I fully understand what you are saying. And I am truly sorry for the loss of your family's matriarch. I send my condolences to you, your husband and his family." J.B. allowed me space and time to grieve. And I fully accepted her kindness. Yes, she was more than a mere editor. She was a humanitarian who loved all people, regardless of their circumstances or status in life.

Sometime later, during my period of lamentation, I became so enraged at God for inflicting me with the parents that I detested. Why had He not provided me with loving, kind, understanding parents? Sure, I acknowledged that children can sometimes be a handful. And they would need to be disciplined for specific incidents of misbehavior. But what could a four-year-old girl do that was so inherently evil that warranted being locked in a tiny closet for hours on end?

These things still haunted me on a daily basis, and I had no idea what the future would hold for me. I still had pent up hatred and anger in me that I was never allowed to release as a child. And there would come a time when that hatred and anger would have to be released in order for me to move ahead in life. But at this present time, I still had much to learn even though I thought I was stable enough already.

J.B. had repeated herself when she would say "The sins of your parents are drenched in guilt. You were their one scapegoat that would not fight back. And you did not fight back because that is exactly how they groomed you to be. They felt powerful when they wielded their supreme prominence of authority to silence you for the rest of your life. Now, this is the time and the place for you to break that silence. Do not continue to cower as if you have been defeated. You may well be the only victorious member of your family because you recognize them for who they really are. This time they cannot escape. So, speak the truth and shame the devil."

Hearing little quips like that made me feel at ease with J.B. She instinctively knew how to approach a person in their own vulnerability. This was the mark of not just an extraordinary editor, but a rare jewel of a friend. People regard friends as those they meet and have special bonds with. J.B. taught me that this is not always the case. Friends can be very close though miles away and never having even met in person. She was a remarkable woman with the quintessential model of dignity and grace. She was the exact opposite of what I was.

Two weeks after my mother-in-law died, J.B. called to check up on me. Exactly like a friend should do. She did not call to talk about the manuscript, but to see if we were all processing our grief and feeling better about our memories of her to help us through the grief.

Always very conscientious about the suffering of others, J.B. quietly, almost solemnly, spoke. "You never get over it. But living with the empty pain gets easier as you accept that your loved one is no longer suffering." Yes, that was it. With all the medical problems she had endured for years, she was finally no longer debilitated from those pains that tormented her in the daily grind that was her life. She had been freed from the multiple illnesses. J.B. could comprehend the rite of passage that we all must cross when we leave this world and enter the next realm.

I thanked J.B. for her caring heart and receded back into my subdued state. I sobbed for the woman I would never see again nor speak to again. But I also intermittently laughed at the happy memories she left for me, my husband and her entire family. Memories of sweeter days when she would say or do something comical that she was not even aware that she was doing. And that, in itself, made the memories even more precious.

One memory came very vividly into my mind, and I had to share it with J.B. I had received some persimmons from a friend and so I decided to make persimmon bread loaves. The whole house smelled like an aromatic bakery. My mother-in-law sent my husband and I to the store to get some milk for her coffee to have with the bread. Upon our return we heard hammering. She did not hear us enter the house because of the loud hammering noise. And we caught her using one of the loaves to hammer a nail into the kitchen counter. She had accidentally dropped one of the loaves on her foot and that is how she found out they were as hard as bricks. When we confronted her about what she was doing, my mother-in-law tried to hide the persimmon loaf behind her back. My husband reached behind her and took the loaf from her hands. We all started laughing.

Later when a nephew stopped by, he delighted in the sweet smell of the persimmon loaves. He asked about them and was told they were as hard as bricks. He tried to be positive about the situation and asked me to make another batch. "I was thinking of putting in a brick walkway in front of my house. I need some bricks."

J.B. laughed so hard that she was left breathless and coughing. After she regained her composure, she recalled a time when she was a newlywed and attempted to make lasagna. "The sauce was perfect, the meat beautifully seasoned, and the pasta fit the baking dish to its exact measurements. There was so much anticipation because the whole house smelled delicious. When Jack and I sat down for a home cooked meal we had bright sunny smiles on our faces. Jack cut the lasagna and we heard a crunch. I had failed to boil the noodles before adding all the other ingredients. I must have suddenly had a look of great disappointment on my face because Jack suddenly scooped some into his mouth and declared it to be the best lasagna he had ever tasted." We both rocked with laughter. Neither one of us started out as good cooks. Miraculously we had both learned from our mistakes and counted ourselves as excellent self-proclaimed chefs from then on.

A couple more weeks went by in a blur, but I was able to put my pen to use. The pages were slow to put out, but they were at least being written. J.B. had not contacted me within those two weeks. She must be busy, otherwise she would have picked up the phone by now. I decided to wait another week before calling her, if she did not contact me first before then. I had known she was a busy woman. Busy with other writers, in her own personal life, and her collaboration work with her colleagues. I was not worried for as each day that passed my concentration on the manuscript was being put out page after page. Chapter after chapter was flowing from the depths of long-ago scenes. I would never have to experience anymore horrors at the hands of anyone.

This type of freedom comes rarely to people like me. Those who have suffered at the hands of someone they trusted, loved, and yearned to be accepted by. Futile as it may seem, this is the life of an unwanted child. And it affects their reasoning as they enter adulthood. And later, if they have children, it will affect them too.

It occurred to me after a few weeks more time that J.B. sounded exhausted when we had last spoken to each other. Her breathing was strained, her voice barely audible, as if she was almost whispering. True her vocal cords elicited soft orations of well-educated expressions. But this seemed different. Still gentle but with a hint of exhaustion. When she would call again, I would ask her if she felt ill. But only if I detected the same labored sounds in her breathing, as it is impolite to ask outright about a person's health when it is not necessary to do so.

Still, it nagged at me, and I kept a diary of sorts to remember the incident, just in case I needed it for future reference. It was one of the most serious decisions I was to make. For later on I was able to refer back to these notes and put pieces of our conversations together like I was putting a puzzle together. Everything fit together as all the clues became evident.

Chapter 10

Not many more weeks stretched on before J.B. dialed up my phone number. Still, that seemed like an eternity to me. And being the doubtful and insecure new writer, I was beginning to worry if J.B. did not call at least once a week. Even though I knew that was an impossibility for her to be at my beck and call each week. By this time, I was beginning to feel as if she had found a more profitable author. Maybe a more established author had come into her view and restricted her time on calls to me. She tried sounding jubilant as she began with her soft sweet French voice.

J, B,: "Bon jour, mon ami"

(Good day, my friend}

Me: "Bon jour, J.B. Ca ma manque de parler avec toi. Comment- allez vous?"

(Good day, J.B. I missed talking to you. How are you?)

J.B.: "Tres bien, merci."

(Very well, thank you}

This was the proper way to answer a person who is not close to you. She did not speak any slang or in a dialect too familiar with the other person.

I had researched on how to properly ask this in French, as I am not fluid in the beautiful French language. I was so limited that I had hoped J.B. would answer in English so I would not have to strain my weak grasp of the language in answering her. I was relieved to hear her continue to answer in English after the pleasantries were done. Had she continued in French I would have had to explain that I did not speak fluent French.

Once again, I heard that she was labored in her breathing. Her answer would not have surprised me if she would have admitted that she was in pain. But J.B. did not say one word that alluded to any kind of health problems. Instead, she insinuated that she was quite healthy, and it was the cold dampness of the New York air that was the issue.

"Anyone who lives in New York can tell you it is a beautiful, bustling town but also cold as a freezer beginning in the latter part of Autumn and continuing throughout the middle of Spring." She struggled to maintain a normal breath, which was quite notable even throughout her denials.

The weather. That is what she was wasting this long distance call on. I had heard of the constant rain in New York and its icy winters. But I had not asked J.B. about weather conditions. Still, I accepted her answer as her wanting privacy about her health. I had been communicating with J.B. for over a year at this time and I instinctively recognized her need for privacy on certain subjects. This was one subject she did not care to discuss. Had I been afforded the consideration to be privy to her condition I most certainly would have pushed myself to the conclusion of that dang manuscript. But for now, I was enjoying our conversations and was wishing they could go on for a lifetime.

So, I took my time in finishing up what should have been an otherwise easy task. After all, I did not have to just sit back for hours on end contemplating imagined dialogue or scenes. They were already at my disposal whenever a memory crept out of its dark crevice. But, if they were not too gruesome, I filed them in the back of my mind as they popped up into the present life that I did not want them invading. I knew they would eventually pop up again.

J.B. bolted me straight back into reality. "I am trying to tell you that if you wait too long, your story may become commonplace and irrelevant. You do not want that to happen. More and more everyday people will tire of abuses similar to what you have experienced. And those people will not be afraid to speak up and stand for justice. Right now, your story is unique. And it may still be unique in twenty years. But that is not a guarantee. Who knows? Maybe in fifty years it will still be relevant, considering the substance and language. You have a keen memory. You have proven that many times over in and throughout our conversations. I do admire intelligence like yours. It makes me more aware of what I say to you because I know for a fact that you may bring up information or a phrase I have accidentally let out." Now I understood why she hesitated to answer some of my questions. She was being cautious about her private life.

J.B. was correct about me on that. It is true that I would jot down inferences and advice she would impart immediately after each phone call ended. Then I would read them over and over again until her words were tattooed into my memory banks. And there they remained. Forever a part of me. Of course, there were times when I threw myself full force into my writing. But more often than not, I did so when I yearned to impress J.B. and not for any real self- satisfaction. I know, not the best reason to keep the script going, but it appeared to be beneficial to me at the time. Procrastination is just a fancy word for laziness. And J.B. was tired of my delaying tactics. She made that very clear to me several times over. Still, she was patient with me.

"You are taking this manuscript too lightly." She began in a stern voice, and I knew I had taken advantage of her patience. "Successful people jump in with both hands and feet to get their work done. This book should have been done and accomplished six months ago. I may have to overlook this fantastic piece of biographical history if you keep refusing to complete it in a timely manner. Now, what do you have so far? Any new chapters? How far from the finished product are you? I need answers now!"

Goodness J.B. could be such a tigress when she did not get her way. Her interest lay within her guidelines of editing and publishing a book that she considered worthy of her time and effort. My stalling stopped her from doing her work as an editor.

She was losing faith in me. I could not let that happen. Assuring her that I had at least two chapters for her to scan over and scrutinize, she became more subdued. My heart raced. This was not like her. Usually, she asked me about the intimate details of the script. Now

J.B. just wanted this project over with and on to the publishing part of the book.

My curiosity peaked. "J.B., is there something you need to tell me about my manuscript? Has Doubleday changed their mind about publishing it? If so, tell me now so I can search for another publishing company." Then I waited for the worst news possible from her.

Ever so slowly J.B. began in almost a breathless quiet tone. "No. do not ever think you have done something wrong. You need only to move along a little faster in your writing. I do not know how else to spur you on. I cannot give you the confidence that you need to continue in this project. I also cannot automatically grant you the courage to finish what you have started. You need to seek the reason why you eve3n began writing this story in the first place. You mentioned it to me once before. Go back to that place in your heart. That place where you decided to begin putting pen to paper. Then you can complete your manuscript. It has always seemed to me that it will be a best seller. By the way, I will not be coming into the office as much as I have been doing. And I do not know how often I will be in, but I will call you as time allows. You can still call and leave a message for me." Short and to the meat of the conversation. No frills or French were involved in this call. And she subtly added the part of not coming into the office as if I would not notice.

I realize now that I should have been able to put it all together at that time. Her words were now always whisper like and they were beginning to get more concise. The phone calls were also shorter. But at the same time, she insisted that she was healthy and that nothing was wrong with her. I knew that to not be the case but what was I to do? Call her an outright liar? I could never do that.

"I am fine." She chimed in suddenly. "Maybe some allergy sniffles but not much more. I just need to conserve my energy, as busy as I am. You are not an exclusive client. There are hundreds of manuscripts that find their way into Doubleday publishing. Not all of them get picked up. And they are of different subjects. When I came across your manuscript, I felt it was well written for an unknown. The flow was superb."

She must have felt as if she was repeating herself, which she was. There was a tired redundancy that was distinctive in her speech. And I knew I had run out of time. Out of excuses. And J.B. was out of patience.

I managed to mumble that I would get the manuscript completed and sent to her within two to three months. If I ran into a roadblock, I promised that I would contact J.B. immediately so as not to waste any more time. I assured her that at this point she had done everything that I needed to have a finished product. She accepted me at my word. I did not have any excuse left that she would or could accept after this. We left it at that and said our goodbyes. I was once again alone.

I had run my course of free advice, patience and guidance. And now I had to glean whatever I could from our conversations and from the numerous notes I had jotted down after our conversations, this eventuality made me remorseful of my selfish behavior. This regret was to follow me the rest of my life.

I only pray I can truly help someone else through my own life experiences. My own mistakes. Healing would have to wait until I could get through this manuscript.

Chapter 11

Contemplating my chances of publication, J.B.'s words hung in the air. "Tomorrow is promised to no one. If your manuscript is to ever become a real published book, then it must be done quickly. Time does not belong to you. It will definitely unfold and tick on and on whether or not you are prepared for its inevitability. The choice or decision, however, are yours. To proceed is invaluable. To prohibit your story from being told is catastrophic."

Yes, I knew full well that I was hanging on by a thread. But did I truly want that kind of negative notoriety? In all fairness I should accept it because in the long run I would get everything out and put it all behind me. Plus, I could enable some others to be courageous enough to help themselves. Maybe some parents would repent and stop their abusive behavior before they permanently damage the souls of their innocent children. This thought scared me. I did not know how to raise my own children. I knew I would make mistakes. Mistakes that I probably should know better. But being a better parent without guidance was going to be difficult.

J.B. was an advocate for abused, neglected, ill or starving kids. Her heart was as soft as her voice. She had traveled all over the world in her quest to aid children abroad as well as domestic.

"Losing a child humbles a person and you develop a sense of protection for those who have no means of protecting themselves. That is one of the many reasons why your work is crucial. You know firsthand exactly how these children feel. You also know how to teach parents on what to do to break that cycle. And that is a lifelong lesson for them to adhere to. Granted, it may not be beneficial to a few. But if that is the case, they will eventually need psychological intervention. Your parents may be at that eventual critical stage."

Once again J.B. was correct on her assessment. I already knew my parents had something off about them that was off the grid of normality. No mother or father should be saying or doing what they did in a normal parent child relationship. Worst of all they had three of their own kids learning the ropes of how to be just like them. Conniving, convincing and dangerous behind closed doors. I, myself was not a perfect mother but I was a long way from being like them.

I was, in fact, accused of spoiling my children too much. Baking goodies for them as after school snacks, allowing them an hour of freedom and rest time immediately after school and letting them jump all over the furniture. J.B. seemed like a good parent. So, I asked her about raising children at the end of one phone call. "J.B., is there such a thing as overindulging and spoiling your kids even if you do not have a bulging bank account? My parents and sisters say I do not discipline my kids enough and they will grow up not amounting to anything."

In her thoughtful manner J.B. answered "Yes, there is a very likely chance that can happen but at lower and slower degree. It may be that because you have encouraged them that they can do anything, they just may be successful in life. Whereas you were conditioned to be submissive, they have that part of you in them to propel themselves to succeed as they wish."

What an extraordinarily intelligent woman J.B. was. I loved all five of my children but did not know how to be a good parent to them.

Did not know how to show it. I was like a temperamental child myself. And many times, I would sorely become overwhelmed by parenthood. I did not always make the best decisions, whether or not I knew better.

J.B. made it clear that all parents make mistakes. "We have all been through that. The doubtful stages will come and go. Just reassure your children that deep down in your heart you love them with all your heart. If they choose to accept that love, then they are more intelligent than what you think. If not, then they must look within themselves to see why they lack empathy."

I suppose there was a too long pause as she continued. "I have made so many mistakes with my own children. But when frustration would set in, I had the good fortune of having a nanny or governess to help me out. According to what you have told me, you have no positive outside structure on which to rely on. So, my friend, I try to bring a more warming order or construction, if I may, into your life. The probability that you may learn from this experience is far greater than your parents ever learning parenting skills at all."

I did finish my manuscript shortly after this last conversation with J.B. fourteen chapters that summed up my life experiences. I found it difficult to recall happy moments. But when I did, I would immediately jot them down. I had to because they were so brief and far between that I had to stretch so far to retrieve them. In my daily routine they were so much easier to access while I was doing the things I enjoyed most, like baking.

The beatings that made me bleed every time, the mental anguish, the physical abuses that also entailed pedophilia and incest were soon to be over in my life. I could let go of it forever. And I could do it in a way that everyone would know why I was the way I was.an odd duck out, strange, different and oh so lonely. I trusted J.B. with the details, and she patiently listened and never judged me. Although I sensed that some of the specifics of my background sickened her, she never interrupted and kept her perspective to herself. My viewpoint is what mattered to her.

"My contention is that you lived this life. You understood it better than anyone else. You also fear it like no other. Think what other kids may feel like under these same conditions. Are their fears as valid as yours are? Do they suppose that it is a normal way of life? Just as you thought it was normal. At least all the tribulations you endured will stand for something pragmatic and productive." J.B. ended this call on a low key. The understanding and advice were there. The guiding voice to which I fully trusted was there also.

J.B.'s calls were rare now. I referred to my never-ending notes of our calls to decide where I should go with my next chapter or even to the next phrase. I was making my own decisions and found that I was quite capable of writing my biography in a smooth and understandable version of my truth. I felt that when I was ready to mail off the next few chapters, they would have a very positive response from J.B. after reviewing them.

Again, I noted that J.B.'s calls were fewer and further between. Maybe it was that she believed she had taught me enough that I could continue on my own without the constant rehearsing of the sane old advice and now she could relax and let go o the reins a little bit.

J.B. had called it confidence in training, but I knew it ran deeper than that. It was my heart being reassured that I could go on living in peace without the maladies of my past. It was at this time that I made the decision to visit my parents and tell them that I forgave them for everything that they had ever said or done against me.

I also informed them that I would not be attending their funerals at the time as whenever they each passed away. My father grunted, cussed at me, then told me to leave his house.

My mother cried and said I was disrespectful for saying that. Really? She had the nerve to speak about respect. Somehow, I found it amusing. I turned to leave, never to see either one of them again.

In the back of my mind, I kept thinking that J.B.'s calls were so rare that it could only be one of two reasons. One, Doubleday Publishing had actually dropped my manuscript because of my lack of timely writing. Or two, she had fallen so ill that she was not able to respond or call as before. She did not sound healthy the last time we had conversed. And they did not last over seven to ten minutes. The only thing that had not changed was the intimacy of our friendship. We had established that bond months earlier. No matter which way the tide turned for my manuscript, our harmony could never be sullied by antagonism.

This leg of my journey was coming to an end. My manuscript was finally completed, and I was ready for it to be reviewed by J.B. and to hear her final opinion of how it turned out. I was not afraid or anxious anymore to hear what she had to say. It hit me like thunder as I realized that I had become confident in my writing skills. Not sure exactly when that happened, but I noticed it now and it felt great. I smiled to myself and the little girl who had just become an adult. And I had J.B. to thank for my newfound status.

I called J.B. and left her a message, confident that I would hear from her within a few days. I wanted to tell her of the good news that I had completed the work that had made me so miserable. A hurdle that had been crossed with that new confidence that I had found only recently. She did not call within those few anticipated days. I left a secondary message for her to call because I had good news for her about my manuscript. Still there was no response.

Not being one to quit now, I decided to wait an entire week to see if she would have a chance to call me. I was very happy about my accomplishments and breakthroughs by this time, so not hearing from her did not diminish my confidence. Even with the two reasons why she did not call crossed my mind several times, I was still hopeful.

Chapter 12

I finally heard from J.B. after another week or so had passed by. I told her excitedly that I had completed eight chapters. Upon her request, I mailed off my work to Doubleday Publishing, in care of J.B. She also had requested that I mail my first four chapters that she had previously edited. I had corrected the one error that she had previously edited and submitted four more chapters for her to peruse at her leisure. I was in no hurry now. I knew I could present her with a completely finished product within weeks.

J.B. was delighted with my level of writing. "I have found no errors in the last four chapters. They are grammatically correct, interestingly written, well documented and congruent. You have stayed true to yourself, even if you did explain your demeanor in a shaded way. No one is perfect but you have admitted your guilt in various situations. Never stray from the truth, although that may encase your own mistakes as well as your parents' and siblings' transgressions. I had secretly hoped that you would not portray yourself as a saint. And you did not do that. That speaks volumes about your character and authenticity. And most of all, your ability to combine them as a successful writer. Remember to not wallow in the world of self-pity. That is so destructive.

And if you let it consume you, you may never recover from it."

J.B.'s accolades were like music to my ears. But yet, the stern warnings chipped away at my nerves. I was at peace with my newfound confidence, and I did not want to hear of anything negative at this joyous time. I took note of her warnings and of our conversation so that I could read it over in my own time, at my own pace. I wanted to be sure to memorize everything that J.B. had warned me about. And I did just that.

The advice, the warnings, the stories that unfolded over our many months of conversations were kept in a notebook that I used as reference during the times when J.B. was not there to help push me along the road to publication. Still, I knew she was only as far as that phone call or message. So now, after mailing off the last chapters to J.B., I waited for the return of my work.

It was two weeks before J.B. returned my manuscript. It was pure delight to see zero corrections on it. Within those two weeks I managed to produce another whole chapter. Slow as this may seem, it is vigorous work. And even more so for a first-time writer not sure of how it is supposed to be done. This amounted to thirteen chapters completed. Maybe I did not finish them in a timely manner, but I did complete them. I would never have done this had it not been for J.B. and her encouragement.

Maintaining a balance between home management and this manuscript work felt like I had two full time jobs. One occupation was a breeze and fun to accomplish. Then I had to sit for my scheduled writing. This was the most difficult aspect of my daily routine. By this time, I had learned to function without J.B.'s weekly calls, as I had implemented all of her advice and guidance from the notes that I had written down. Not that it was any easier without her calls.

She had imparted as much wisdom as she possibly could without compromising either the writing or the developed friendship. We had never met in person, but we were both inclined to agree that this was a most unusual meeting of minds that we would treasure forever. Without a doubt I instinctively knew that it did not matter who came into and out of our lives. This was an unusual friendship, yes. But a friendship, nonetheless. J.B. treated everyone with the utmost courtesy and respect. And she never asked for anything more in return. She was truly a lady who deserved that respect.

It was effortless to fall under her spell. She exhibited qualities of educated well-mannered dedication to those she came into contact with. She left me speechless many times over and I admired her for that. J.B. did what an excellent editor was meant to do. She roped in publishing possibilities and did so in a timely fashion while extending a helping hand to get the work to a stage of published finality.

This is the stage where I was at for the moment. Twelve chapters was my goal, possibly an extra two just to satisfy myself that this was truly complete with the most pertinent parts included. I was eight chapters deep into my writing.

Plus, I had the first four original chapters and an extra one already done. I was past my goal at this point. The memories came faster and faster now as I sat and wrote each one as fast as they erupted. Memories that no longer frightened me into submission were welcomed into the manuscript. This was my breakthrough. Of course, J.B. already knew it would come in its own time. She counted on it. Yes, it was effortless to appreciate her with all her patience and encouragement.

Echoes of her calls came to light as I well understood that her calls would soon diminish as other authors would take my place in her editorial endeavors. I considered myself to be one of the lucky ones who could embrace her wisdom and counseling. And most of all, I would take away with me, the beautiful friendship of someone I had never met. Unusual and yet unique.

Just about the time I was completing the tenth chapter of that dreadful manuscript, I left a message for J.B. notifying her of the extra two chapters that I felt were necessary for the story to be complete and accurate. It would be more than a week before she responded.

And there it was again. That distinctive laboring of breath that was by now familiar to me and recognizable. She tried to keep confident in her ability to mask any health problems. "Please excuse my weariness. I guess time has ravaged my poor old body. But do not worry about any supposed illnesses. What would an extra two or three chapters entail? She smoothly transitioned the subject over to my book.

I caught it. Her subtleness was not well hidden very well. There were long awkward pauses as she regained her breath and strength to continue. The little lilt in her voice was absent. I shuddered back an unnerving wavering feeling of despair. She was slipping away from me and I blamed myself for stringing along a manuscript that she believed in.

I explained that the extra chapters would entail my present life and how I needed to let my children know that although I was not an ideal mother, I loved them, even if I did not know how to express that love.

J.B. explained her own misgivings about how she had raised her children as well. "I have made so many errors of judgement throughout my years of parenthood. But I am lucky that my son and daughter have forgiving hearts." J.B.'s children were wise, intelligent and understanding. But above all of this they were forgiving. And that was the catalyst for becoming a successful and mature adult. People who adhere to forgiveness know how to keep families intact and loving.

"Rewards come sparingly" J.B. had once told me. "And the time to reflect on why you achieve these rewards is unfairly short."

"I do not understand what that means" I replied. I always felt so inadequate whenever I talked to J.B. because of my limited education.

"It means that with all the despair and nightmare of a life you have been witness to for your whole life, your reward will amount to only this book. But I assure you that it will undoubtedly last far longer than the years you suffered in your lifetime. That is the sparingly part. The reflecting part will be much shorter in time, as I suspect your style of writing will be in such great demand. You will not have time reflect for very long before publishers will want you to collaborate with them on either a sequel or on another project. You will not have time to reflect on your past hurts, shame or your parents' picadilloes. When it is your time to shine, let it only be for a brief moment in time while you excel in other work or projects."

J.B. had encouraged me enough during our conversations, but I was struck silent when she pondered what my literary abilities could entail. "If there is even remotely a chance, maybe in the future, you might consider applying yourself as an editor. Your skills are acutely reminiscent of great authors who have become literary editors themselves and even greater authors because of their finite editing."

There it was. Her absolute trust in my writing talent. My silence must have been a solidly clear indication to her of my shock. I believed thy the only reason my manuscript was even halfway presentable was because J.B. had coached me along the entire way. When I said just that, she lightly giggled and said "No, my dear friend, I only encouraged you to shine in your own way. Your ability to do so was already there, just waiting to burst forth from you so you could apply it."

Chapter 13

Conversations with J.B. seemingly left me mystified. How long had she been thinking of my writing abilities on terms of the future? I just had to ask. "J.B., how long has it been since you first started thinking of my writing in terms of a future in that business? Especially when you consider that I am an unknown."

"Calm down, M.S." she chortled. "I noticed the command of the vocabulary with your first four submitted chapters. But then, there are hundreds of amazing writers that I have seen over the years. So, after I read over the secondary set of chapters, I knew there was a more important impact you could have in the literary field."

She had secretly assessed what I could be worth, not only to myself but to other struggling authors, if I should ever become an editor.

J.B. was looking out for my future. In her unselfish way, she went beyond what an editor should have done for someone just starting out in the literary world. One where I could excel in. I danced around the room after that phone call and jotted down each and every word she had said so it could be engrained in my memory. I read it so many times over I could recall it like I could recall my own name.

Knowing I was touching on the last couple of chapters, J.B. reminded me that I needed an intro to my book. A prologue she had said. Also, I was to write an epilogue and more terms that I did not understand. "After you are satisfied with your last chapter you must go back and write a sort of introduction as to what the book is about. That, in literary terms, is a one-to-five-page outline of book."

Okay, so now I understood the term prologue. "So, I have to write somewhat of a book report to let the audience know what they are getting into so to speak. A book report, really? This seemed a ridiculous idea. Still, I wrote down all of the extra items and extra page that I was now expected to complete.

"Exactly! J.B. exclaimed. "Now the epilogue is just the opposite of the prologue. It is a comment or a conclusion to what has just been read. It ties up loose ends that were left in question throughout the book."

I had to repeat it as I understood it, while writing down everything she instructed me on. "Okay, so if the reader is left confused about an area or a chapter within the book, the epilogue will clarify it. In other words, I need to tell the reader the ending of the book."

J.B. was clear in her explanation. But I just wanted to make sure I did fully understand what she was so desperately trying to convey.

"Right on point again" she answered in her now obvious out of breath response. She regained her composure then continued in a slow, calculated demeanor. Her every word had to be concise as she tired easily now and had no time for repeating anything.

"There should be a page or two to thank those who may have contributed to the making of the book. This part is known as the book's acknowledgements. It comes right before the prologue. It can be about those who gave emotional, physical or financial support to you during the manuscript phase. You, as the author, acknowledge their contribution and thank them for doing so as a collaborative effort."

When I questioned her about the physical part, J.B. laughed and simply said it was anyone who helped me write or type up the manuscript. Not having a computer, I did all my typing at the local library by myself. So, I asked about that. It turns out that this page could possibly be eliminated if I did all the writing, typing and printing up of my manuscript without any help whatsoever from anyone.

Underscoring this, J.B. made sure to let me know that this was not the dedication page. What? Another page? Her advice was always heeded by trust. But now here were at least another eight to ten pages I would need to fulfill the necessary requirements of an updated, completed manuscript. What more was there to befall me? Furiously I wrote down all that she was now saying I was required to complete. Even though I repeatedly asked her to explain some of the things over and over again, she did so without constraint. She even asked if I was writing down all the specifics that she was stating. It was that important to her that I jot it all down word for word.

"This page is usually just one page and is set before the book even begins. This is the author's special mention in a separate thank you to only a certain person or group. This is an honorary page. It is short and more personal. Unlike the acknowledgement page, which is lengthier and may include your editor." She slightly chuckled at this idea as well as I did. I knew I would be including J.B. as well as others. The manuscript would not have ever been completed without her.

"Now, getting back to the dedication page, it comes immediately after the title page. The acknowledgements are generally at the end of the book."

Oh my gosh! Now J.B. added a title page. When was she going to stop adding pages? But I kept writing down all of the necessary information so that I could at last be done with this manuscript. This seemed like an insane thing to be doing. I felt that if a person reads the book, then they should understand what it was they were reading. I did not want to write a summarized book report.

"You're adding a title page?" I was getting mighty frustrated with

J.B. and with all the additional pages and their fancy little names. I wanted to be done with this phase of the manuscript already. J.B. knew what she was talking about. I merely did not want to go the extra mile to have it completed as she instructed. I was being overwhelmed again by this seemingly never-ending story. I was on a merry go round and could not find a way off. And still she droned on. My head hurt but J.B. did not cease to add more and more pages to this madness.

"Yes. A well written book has a title page" J.G. explained to my feeble little mind.

"Do people not know what they are reading by the title on the cover? In my heart I was imploring her to stop adding pages.

"Of course, they do. But, as I said, a well written book includes a title page. By the way, acknowledgements may be listed at the beginning of the book, or either before or after the table of contents page. She thought she had thrown that last one out on a sly note. Like I was not going to notice another additional page.

"Another page? My fully frustrated brain was on fire, and I feared I would take it out on J.B. although I did not want to. She was the one person fiercely fighting for me to succeed. So, I kept on making her repeat herself until I could write it all down correctly. I struggled but eventually got it all down. J.B. made me read it all back to her to ensure that she was content that I was understanding it fully.

"Now, as far as the table of contents" J.B. began quickly and breathlessly. I knew she had more hidden page requirements. "Can be listed simply as table of contents or TOC and is located on the page immediately before the start of the first chapter. It contains the titles of each chapter along with the chapter's first page number. This is advisable for works of nonfiction style, as yours is. She tried to sound upbeat and reassuring. But her tattered sounding breathing gave way to a totally different expression. One of weakness and in need of rest. But here she was. Starting yet another page. A table of contents, as she had mentioned.

Well, got through all the additional pages. Or so I thought. J.B. still had more on her mind. I thought to myself when will the madness end? So much more went in to writing a book than I had originally anticipated. And the additional work, or pages, amounted to another chapter to write. Another chapter that was required before I submitted my manuscript for publication.

"There is finally the inclusion of photos to address." J.B. had to inhale sharply in order to continue the conversation. A conversation that I felt was already passed its limitations on requirements. "Photo pages are not generally numbered, although they are counted. For example, you have a written page that is numbered thirty-five. Next are four pages of photos. They are numbered thirty-six through thirty-nine. Your next numbered written page is forty. When you send in your completed manuscript, make sure it is numbered as so. I know, this is somewhat confusing. In a book of non-fiction, it just might be more compelling to number the photo pages. And be diligent about including a few words or one sentence about each photo."

Oh my gosh. Now I had to briefly describe any photos and decide if I want those pages numbered. Not genuinely wanting to know the answer, in a beleaguered tone I inquired if there was anything else I had to be aware of before mailing off my finished manuscript. A manuscript that was hopefully soon to be published, according to

J.B. "Anything else?" I meekly asked.

"Yes, there is one more thing." J.B. became happy at the thought that I had asked for more information. But, oh no, I just had to ask, didn't I? "Please contact me the minute you have a final product and have fun summing up those worn-out treads of your life."

J.B. had no idea how relieved I was to hear those precious words. The finality of it was so clearly evident. Even her labored breath seemed to bring about more enthusiasm in her voice. As we concluded this phone conversation, I was left feeling overwhelmed with all that I needed to get accomplished before mailing back the manuscript. It had been approximately one and a half years since I began my conversations with J.B. and almost two years since I first began my self-therapy in recollecting my childhood.

Chapter 14

After the mountain of information about the addition of several more pages that J.B. stated were necessary, I felt that I would never finish this manuscript in its entirety. I went over the pages she had mentioned.

A prologue, which was an introduction to the book. How was I ever going to introduce severe child abuse and witchcraft in a single page for everyone to understand? J.B. had said it was more of an introduction to the book. To allow the reader to know what to expect when they read the entire book itself. There was also the option to have a qualified literary person or magazine to state a few sentences to add to the reading value of a published book. They do not have to read the book in its entirety, maybe a few chapters will be sufficient to assess their statements.

I knew no one in the literary field nor anyone who was associated with a reputable magazine. This was more like a school homework assignment where I would have to research magazines that made literary statements. I would also have to find someone who would be willing to make a brief statement to justify reading my published book. This assignment would be the difficult part to achieve after the story had already been told in my manuscript.

The epilogue was my statement. A somewhat summing up of the facts that were within the book. This would be much easier I surmised, as I knew every word in the manuscript, so I would or should know how to summarize it. J.B. had warned me about not going over the page amounts for each of the prologue and epilogue. Too much of each would diminish the storyline as opinions may be inserted instead of actual fact. Too little of each would imply that the story itself would make for a boring book. A summary of my life could not be established within a few pages. But after J.B.'s cautionary remark, I was left to my own devices as to how to approach this section of the book.

I was not privy to the basics of how to go about writing the epilogue within the confines of the literary field guidelines. This would end up being another school homework assignment. I would have to learn how to write about what I had already written. I smiled at this one because I felt like I would be making a book report on my own book.

The acknowledgement page was going to a short page. Very few people helped me to complete this venture. And even less people knew that it existed. This was only because I did not trust anyone with their judgment of the literary field or with any of my childhood secrets. I only hoped that someday I would be brave enough to let my story be known by everyone. Wanting to stay anonymous was one reason I did not have anyone help me with the writing or the typing of the manuscript.

The dedication page is where I made a personal choice as to whom I wanted to be immortalized in my book. They would not necessarily be instrumental in the writing or typing or any other help in the construction of any part of the manuscript. This is where I could make a loved one shine. in this page. It did not matter if the person was even dead or alive. All that mattered was that I would want to include them as a part of my special acknowledgement just for being in my life and making me a better person. A person who ultimately was capable and courageous enough to write about the sins of my family.

Now about that title page. This page bears the title of the book.it also includes the name of the author, publisher, place of publication and sometimes the date of publication. This bit of information seemed irrelevant because when a person picks up a book, the first thing they see on the cover is the title of the book. The second thing they notice is the author's name. why would a reader open up the book only to read the same title and same author's name? Redundant. The only thing different was that the reader could be informed of all the little details of how the book came about being published.

It was only after J.B. finished adding pages, did I finally ask her to clarify some of the extra work that I was expected to automatically know how to do. School homework without instruction. All J.B. did was to repeat what she had already instructed me to do. She then asked me to read back what she had said and wanted me to verify that I understood the instructions clearly. She had no time to keep going back, step by step, in her final instructions. J.B. felt it imperative that I understood now. She would be leaving for a longer time, and she would not be able to contact me as often as she had been doing. It occurred to me that she was letting me out on my own so I could truly learn by doing the work by myself.

The only trouble with that is that I did not know where to begin. And J.B. did not tell me step one on how to go about collecting all the information required to do it. J.B. had told me to research what she had told me needed to be done.

"Look at several books in your local library and see how they are put together as a finished product. Find where the prologue, epilogue and all the rest of the pages are situated. Copy down their examples and go from there."

Research is what I had not had to do throughout the manuscript because everything was already in my memory banks. I did not know how I was going to do it, but it seemed easy enough the way J.B. had said to do it. But which area should I start with? That was up to me. Again, where to start was my problem.

Now there was the issue of the table of contents page. Also referred to as TOC. This meant that each chapter had its own identity marker. If the reader looked over this page, they could easily identify what the chapter as about. The page number where any chapter began was visible but not where it ended.

This meant that I would need to go back and sum up what each chapter entailed. Then give it a title. Now the reader could go to whatever chapter they wanted to read and on what page to find it. This manuscript was more work than I envisioned. The more chapters I wrote, the more I would have to sum up for the table of contents.

I was curious as to whether or not this particular page was necessary for the book. "J.B. is it necessary to name each chapter? What if the chapters are just numbered?"

Her breathless response was even more labored as she became more frustrated with my every question. It was not that I meant to frustrate her or cause any stress or worry, but I truly was not sure of what I was supposed to do. I had nowhere to turn. J.B. was my only hope. I had to get all this new information right or possibly run the risk of being dropped from consideration by Doubleday Publishing.

This would be a monumental achievement because I knew no one in the literary business nor did I know of anyone in the magazine publishing business. If ever there was a lost sheep, it was me at this moment in time.

I had no leads and no idea where I could get a lead to get any of these new pages completed. There was the possibility I could wing a few pages. But then I would be stuck right back where I was. This did not seem to be going anywhere. there just was not enough instruction for me to move forward. I was so lost and confused and needed J.B.'s help. Even as I tried to do it on my own, she must have known it would be difficult for me to move ahead. I hated to bother her as I felt she was ill, despite her silence on the subject. But the time came when I had to make the decision to call her once more.

I called J.B.'s number again and left a message for her to call me back as I was having trouble getting the pertinent material for the additional pages. The manuscript was at a standstill. I waited a week, but she never called back. I left a second message, still not worried over the time spam since we last had a conversation. I had done as much as I could and was now on the picture pages.

I did not want to do this area of the book as I felt it was an invasion of my privacy. If someone looked at the scars on my face and body, they would automatically know it was me in those pictures. But I also remembered J/B/'s warning abut the ravages of time diminishing those scars. Not only did I have to describe what the reader was already looking at, but I had to add a date and how I got the scars. There was also the matter of telling where I got each of them.

All the while I had to be cognizant of how many pages they would take up and then remember to keep them as somewhat silent pages that were not actually numbered. I wondered if it would be possible to just have a few pictures and have then numbered as I would be filling in a full description of each one as presented on the page. Maybe we could work something out. And if I were allowed to do so, then I would be more apt to have pictures inserted into that middle area of the book itself.

As brilliant of an idea that I thought I had, J.B. did not answer my messages. So, I left a third message. It was mot like her to not answer. After another week I left another message. If she did not call back, I would assume that I was dropped from consideration from Doubleday publishing and I would move on to another publishing company. There, I would start all over again but at a much wiser level because of all that J.B. had taught me about the literary field.

Chapter 15

I was handed a sense of illusion when I first began this trek with J.B. at times it dragged on slowly like an ant hauling a semi-truck. In other instances, the writing flew by so quickly like a military jet trying to break the sound barrier. In either case I had to relive each moment. Sometimes that meant reliving an entire scene several times over while I tried to write it all down before it passed. If I could not get it the first time or the second time, I had to relive it over and over until I got it all purged.

This was an arduous assignment at best because the memories that were relived over and over caused me to have nightmares almost nightly. And severe headaches almost daily. I required instruction from J.B. Yes, I had written down all she had instructed. And yes, I told her that I understood. And I did for the most part. But there were still some parts of the additional pages that mandated more clarification. At least in order for me to continue.

I remembered a time when I had left a message for J.B. it was early. one morning and I had expected a call back from her within two to three days. Instead, it took her almost two weeks to respond. Her calls were spreading put far. This concerned me as the last time she did that she came back sounding fatigued and breathless. I could tell there was more to it than the allergies she claimed to have. Still, I did not question it. I should have.

"Did you have a question dear?" there was that exhausted tone again. This time it seemed more pronounced than ever. She was almost hard to understand, and I strained to hear what she was saying. Yet again she denied being anything but bogged down with a lot of editing work. But I knew better. I could tell this was not the case. This sounded more like respiratory health issues, but I vowed not to press J.B. for any details whether or not my suspicions were founded. I felt she would tell me the complete story in due time. Her due time.

I put away any questions I had about her health and continued "I only want to know if the prologue has to be a maximum of five pages and can direct dialogue be use here."

"Direct dialogue or small quote from the book is useful in grabbing the attention of the reader. It is what the audience can expect to encounter from reading the book. When I read the introduction to a book, I marvel at the way it unfolds in the actual body or content of the story. It is that initial prologue that captures the eye of the reader. Finding it within the chapters gives an aha moment. It is always however not a good idea to go over the five-page limit. Somehow like driving. If it is posted at five miles per hour, then do not go fifty miles per hour." J.B. laughed at her own wittiness, and I just had to laugh along with her.

"Okay then, okay. That was all I needed. Thank you for clarifying that with such visual examples." I was still trying to hold back the laughter from her little examples.

"If you need more such examples just call back into the office. It may take me a while, but I promise you that I will call back." J.B. was also still laughing.

This part of the book, without realizing it, also came with its own setbacks. The memories I had to relive on my own in solitary suffering. So many setbacks getting over those hurdles. Had it not been for the cruelty of my parents, this manuscript would never have been written. Should I thank them for that? No. my only thought was to thank J.B., for she was the only one who had ever taken interest in my story. My life. The life that almost never was because of the many severe beatings and strangulations.

Never did she attribute any of those abuses to me. In fact, her assessments were that as a four-year-old child, I was not to blame for the onset of what was later deemed normal behavior on the part of my parents. Their money kept them safe in society. So, no, there would be no accolades for them. No acknowledgements that would consider them to be a part of my own accomplishments. True, they had everything to do with all of the various punishments. But they had nothing to do with my successes as a writer. And write I did. All of their dirty laundry was going to be let out to dry.

No. there were others more worthy of being mentioned. Wow! I could cut them out of my life just as easily as they cut me out of their lives. And more importantly, I could do so on my own terms. Publicly. And with truth and dignity.

By the time J.B. got around to calling again I had started to ask my godmother for pictures or memories of her own to verify my accounts. She had several stories to recount, and I placed those incidents amongst J.B.'s advice and pearls of wisdom. These all went into accounts and incidents alongside what two aunts and an uncle imparted to me. With all of this I was able to get a full rounded picture of what my parents' background was.

J.B. had many times suggested that I ask relatives to corroborate my recollections within the chapters. I was not surprised to find my mother's direct relatives more than willing to corroborate my memories. I should have listened to her at those times when I needed them to help me out in my endeavors. Now I really needed them now more than ever.

How fascinating to have others so willing to aid me on this because they knew or were witness to the atrocities, I befell at the hands of my parents. And when they did not witness, they heard about from other cousins or aunts. Where J.B. got her ideas to do such thing as to boldly ask the relatives for their input was beyond me.

"As dreadful as your parent's backgrounds sound, there must be at least one relative who can corroborate your story and give much needed input where your own memory may fail you." Her suggestion was a stroke of genius. It hit the jackpot when I asked few of my relatives to help me out.

When I relayed their stories to J.B., she admitted that it made her blush. The details of their recollections were inserted into the manuscript.

"Oh, my goodness. That is way more than what you expected. Not something you would have known as a child. Maybe that was your saving grace. Not having to deal with that at such a tender age." J.B. was appalled at the thought of what I had just heaped upon her shoulders. Not that she was immune to such details. She almost whispered that she knew of infidelities that had occurred in marriages but preferred to not discuss those details. "They are quite embarrassing for all whether they are living or deceased. I prefer not to judge. But people find out anyway and then media get involved. Oh, the mess infidelity creates."

Hmm. Had J.B.'s husband been unfaithful? This was not a subject I cared to approach. After all, she had said he was deceased. That night I went over the notes I had taken, as I always did. There was something I could not quite figure out. I read my notes to the point of getting a massive headache. But I still felt I was missing cues.

Not about the manuscript but rather something more personal. Something about J.B. that I could not figure out. It could have been that I was too naive to appreciate the clues tucked into and within the volumes of notes. When my headaches subside, I will look over them again. Maybe I will catch what I am searching for. But I was not meant to learn what the secrets of my notes held. At least not at that time.

It would all be revealed to me soon enough. And in a most unconventional way. For the here and now my concentration was on my soon to be published book. My thoughts swirled at the way J.B. had suggested I was good enough to be an editor. Continuing with memories forced me to put any future ventures on the back burner.

And of all things, I forgot to ask J.B. about the photos page. How could I have forgotten to ask her about something I was clearly struggling with? Now I was going to have to wait for another two or three weeks before I could venture into that conversation with her. With little patience, I knew I would be calling J.B. before the two weeks were up. All I had to cling to was what little information she granted me from our last call. I had missed an opportunity to expand on the other things that were plaguing me about all the additional pages she had mentioned. I decided to write down my questions ahead of time before reaching out to her again.

I decided to also be more diligent in our conversations so as not to be side stepped by J.B. in her ability to change the topic of discussion or to ignore some of my concerns. Two weeks. I would allow two weeks to pass by to call and leave another message for her to call me. I would be ready with my exact questions in hand so as not to be persuaded to go in another direction. I made copies of my questions and pinned them up in my bedroom, living room and in the kitchen. Whenever she would call. I would be ready, no matter what room I was in when that call came through.

I left a message for J.B. and figured it would take her about two weeks to reply. Three weeks passed. Four weeks passed. After a month I left another message for her to call me.

Little did I know I would never speak to my friendly editor ever again. And those back burners would lose their flame of desire to proceed with my manuscript. The revelation of this hit me like a ton of bricks.

Chapter 16

Time is a funny thing. When you wait for something, time consumes you and it goes by slowly. When you have to complete a school homework assignment on a Sunday night and you have not written word one yet, it goes by way too fast.

I was at that crossroads when time dragged on; I had not heard from J.B. in over a month. I had chalked it up to my not getting my manuscript out in a timely fashion and I had been dropped by Doubleday Publishing. I did not believe J.B. herself had expelled me from the likes of being a published author. I felt that this time it was beyond her reach to keep me on as a potential author. Someone else had obviously made that decision for her.

My story was great, she had said. But my presentation was not professional enough to warrant a contract because I was not able to produce a completed manuscript in a professional way. Being a newcomer to this profession had been tedious for me and I did not know how to present myself as a serious writer. But J.B. had shown a genuine interest in my writing and made me believe' that I could accomplish it in due time. Her understanding of my situation had been far more than I ever expected or even deserved.

So many regrets now swirled in between thoughts of failure and the pursuit to go on. I did, however, have a manuscript. All I needed was the tiniest bit of clarification on the added pages, especially that photo page. It was going to be strange to have another editor look at my manuscript and pass judgement on it. How I needed J.B. at this moment. Now more than ever I knew I was within reach of my goal. My future as a writer was on thin ice.

But I also knew that I had done this to myself. J.B. did all she could and now I was facing the possibility of having to go to another publisher if I ever wanted to make J.B. proud of my work. The knowledge was there now. All the instructions were there. The only thing missing was J/B.'s soft voice telling me what to do step by step.

Regrets of all the times I wasted my and J.B.'s time. My selfish need to continue talking to her almost every week must surely have been the reason for the no contact I was experiencing now. At the time when a person feels they need an extra something, that hunger drives them to the point of oblivion from everything else in their life. I could have, should have taken this venture more seriously. But here I was standing at the crossroads of regret and disillusionment.

Regret is generally defined as being repentant or disappointed. That definitely described me. I repented for being so haughty and with the air of feeling entitled to all the phone calls I could get from J.B.'s conversations. A loathing came to my soul as I longed to start over again. I would not waste J.B.'s time nor her valuable assets.

And as the saying goes regret begets disappointment. I had disappointed J.B. o more than one occasion. Actually, I had disappointed her throughout our conversations. I had put forth little effort while enjoying the benefits of learning valuable lessons. Lessons that someone else would be eager to adhere to, I merely squandered. Such selfishness. As these thoughts came up one by one, there was the endless thought that by losing a contract with Doubleday Publishing, I may not even get picked up by any other publisher. There would be consequences for my being too slow of a writer.

There was always the chance that I would be labeled a bad choice because I could not complete a single manuscript within almost two years' time. Why had J.B. not contacted me to at least give me the reason why she had stopped calling so abruptly? I had so many unanswered questions. I thought I knew J.B. better than that.

Maybe she was not being completely truthful in her assessment of my work. She might even have regrets of her own. In either case, it did not seem natural for her to just disappear without a word. I had to know the real reason for her silence. So, I called and left a message for her to call me. I did not say I was having a problem with the manuscript. Just a simple message for her to call me whenever she had time. I also included that time was not of the essence, I knew she was three hours ahead of me so if she happened to call me at nine in the morning, her time in New York, it would be only six in the morning for me in California. That may seem a perilous time to be answering phone calls, but I was undaunted by the time restraints. So, whenever J.B, called I answered. She too was careful not to disturb me at too early an hour it was a common courtesy that we both abided by,

The nagging thought that J.B. had not answered any of my last few phone calls kept me at odds about what was happening in New York. The thought of starting all over again was not a pleasant thought whatsoever. Yet, I knew I had to do it. I had to break the fear of going on without J.B. and Doubleday Publishing. Slowly I began to seek out other publishing companies. But it seemed like every person I spoke to was cursory at best. None of them seemed to have the same feel or atmosphere that I had experienced with J.B. at Doubleday Publishing. Now it was I who was saying that I would call them back about my manuscript. This was a very dull time for me, and I could not imagine how to approach them either.

I began having horrendous headaches. I could, at times, feel my blood pressure soar. My vision blurred and I sometimes could not drive to pick up my children from school.it was on those days that I would walk to their schools to gather them up and head home for their snacks. Only then did I not think about J.B., the manuscript or the fact that she was not interacting with mw anymore.

But then the next day would arrive, and I could only think of that darn manuscript. There was no mistaking that J.B. had broken contact with me. I felt like a failure. And I felt like I had failed J.B. and Doubleday Publishing. I had to look internally to see what I had learned from her so as not to make the same mistake with other publishers and editors. She still did not call.

Somewhere I mustered up the courage to send my manuscript to another publisher. It was a Christian based company so I thought I would have more success with them. I received my manuscript back within a week. I thought I had hit the jackpot. It had taken Doubleday Publishing twice that amount of time to contact me. And an even longer time to return my first four chapters. Subsequent chapters also took a long time to be returned to me. So, this early return gave me hope for a literary future. I was not scared to open this envelope up as I had been previously from Doubleday.

With eagerness to see how well they accepted my manuscript; I opened the large manilla envelope with my manuscript intact within it. I felt no queasiness to alarm me of anything. If anything, I felt elation surge through me because I knew I had written it quite well, as J.B. had told me many times over. And since I had previously been well accepted at Doubleday Publishing, I knew for certain that this publisher would see my work as clear and fitting to be published.

I was almost smiling as my fingers removed the manuscript from the envelope.at a quick glance at the pages I saw there were no corrections. That was a good sign. Right? Then I came to the letter that was within the envelope. It was in its own separate business size envelope. I happily opened it too with nimble fingers. It was cream colored and had the publisher's symbol on it. I thought it was made even more beautiful because it had a Christian symbol on it. I removed the letter from within carefully.

The first words I read shocked me. It was a letter to inform me that my manuscript was too graphic in nature. The language was something they did not approve of. The content of the story was near blasphemous and not ideal for publishing.at least not at their company. It further stated that they wished me luck on finding a publisher willing to print something as horrifying as my life story. The letter reminded me that they were a Christian publishing company that would never publish anything of that nature.

I was floored by this refusal. I wondered if they had read more than a few pages. The letter had said that I represented the worst of all manuscripts they had ever received. Not the actual writing. They marveled at the beauty of the style of writing. There was no problem with that. But they were appalled at the content of the story.

Well, what about the content? It was a factual piece about an abused girl who had lived to tell her story. A girl who had overcome such tragedy. What about that? Maybe they misunderstood what value the manuscript had. How it could help others who were in the same or similar situations. As

Christians would they not want to help someone else? This was puzzling to me that they would refuse to acknowledge the benefits of such a manuscript.

All of a sudden, I became enraged that they would find my manuscript not worthy of being a publishable piece. I knew it was good work because I read the entire manuscript after I had completed it for J.B. and Doubleday Publishing. And I found it to be as interesting as any published author's writing.

I waited until the following Monday to call them and ask specifically why I was turned down when my writing was in excellent form. I was met with a curt response of, as Christians, they could not possibly print and distribute such a violent and vulgar piece of trash. It would be a sin for them to publish such horror. I needed J.B. but she still was not answering my messages.

This was at the time when a person could contact a publishing company. A time when you could interact with an editor without the use of a literary agent. All one had to do was mail their manuscript directly to the Submissions Office of whatever publishing company. This is what I had done with Doubleday Publishing of New York.

Chapter 17

It was a cool and breezy day in early May 1994. So much sunshine but not the kind that bears down on a person. It was gentle. A caressing type of sunshine. It had been a few months since I had spoken to J.B., and I longed to hear her sugary sweet voice. The voice of an angel I had once said. That description befitted her so perfectly. And although it had been months since I had last heard it, my memory recalled her pitch and inflection with acute accuracy.

I decided to give her another call. It was all I could do to keep from crying. The memory of our last conversation came sharply to my mind. Every word was still just as fresh in my memory banks as if we had just gotten off the line a few hours ago. I missed our conversations. I missed her.

I finally had the courage to leave a message for her as I had so many times before. Again, no response. Even after a week I held out for the hope of her calling me back. It never happened. This time I did not hold back the tears. I let my sorrow overcome me and I sobbed for a couple of hours nonstop. I cried out for the one person who had believed in me. The one person who gave me the strength to go on. And I knew that no matter what publishing company I would eventually end up with, I would include my friend in the acknowledgements.

After that last call, and waiting for a week, I vowed to keep calling on a weekly basis until she answered and could give me a response to my solitary question. Why? Why had she refused to answer my calls and messages for these past couple of months. For some reason I just needed to know why. My rage and pain would not let it be. I had to find out. I would not quit until I had the answer to that question.

There is a saying that says to be careful what you wish for. It just might come true but not in the way you would expect. The day finally came when I called, and a gentleman answered J.B.'s line. The words he said became emblazoned in my heart and memory. After identifying myself he began to explain J.B.'s absence without identifying himself.

I wrote down what he said even as he was talking to me. I thought I was owed an explanation, so I wanted to document everything he had to say. This was what I did each time J.B. would call me. I had attached an ink pen to the lower part of the phone cord long ago. It was my way of being assured that I always was ready to write at any time that J.B. called. The following is a summary of what this stranger related to me. Not exact dialogue but close enough.

As soon as he answered I said "Hello, my name is M.S. and I was looking to speak with J.B., my editor. I have questions about my manuscript."

He answered in somewhat of a shocked tone. "Excuse me? Have you not heard? It's been all over the news media, television, radio and newspapers around the world."

"What are you talking about? I just called to update my manuscript, but I first have questions that need to be answered."

In my confusion my retort came out a little too forceful and I had to apologize for being so abrupt. He still did not answer my question. He was too full of the media's response to something tragic. He was not listening to me or my questions as to why I had called Doubleday Publishing and J.B. in the first place.

Calmly he asked me if I knew who my editor was. Too calmly. Almost in a calculated manner. "Do you know who your editor was? Her real identity?"

With all the dignity I could muster, I coolly responded. "Of course, I know who my editor is. I have been communicating with J.B. for almost two years."

When he next spoke, I could almost imagine him smirking. "Your editor was Mrs. Jacqueline Bouvier Kennedy Onassis. She oft times used only her initials so people would not get wrapped up in her real identity. Apparently, you two formed a bond without any of the idol frills that come with it. Mrs. Onassis passed away in her sleep this morning at her home in New York City, New York.

Dumbstruck does not convey the waves of shock I felt at that moment of truth. Her initials, J.B., immediately became clear. Her wanting to keep our relationship on an even keel. A true friendship was what she was seeking, not one of convenience or idol worship.

How I felt like a fool for not picking up on all the clues she left me. Her first husband being killed in Texas, the dates of significant times in her life. My own greed for becoming a published author prevented me from going beyond my manuscript. Now I had to repent for being such a selfish person.

The man's voice brought me back to reality. "I deeply regret to inform you of this. If you check any local news media, you will see that all that I have told you is the absolute truth."

I thanked the stranger and gave my deepest condolences for the loss of his beloved coworker. There was a long awkward silence before the man asked if I was okay. I said I was deeply saddened but I was okay. I asked if there was anything I could do for him to help ease his pain. He answered in the negative. Another awkward moment of silence passed. Neither one of us knew what to say to the other.

Suddenly I began to sob uncontrollably, and I had to break the conversation. He understood, gave his condolences and we hung up. On a much quieter solemn note than when we began for my anger had subsided. I held the receiver for a minute or so after our conversation ended. I somewhat did not want the conversation to end because I did not want it to be real. I prayed that all his words were lies. or some kind of mistake.

Wanting to know if it was all true made me come out of that trancelike state. I hurried to turn the television set on. Sure enough, there it was. Every station was broadcasting the death of former First Lady, Jacqueline Bouvier Kennedy Onassis. there were her initials, J.B., looking at me right on the screen. I never associated her with being someone other than my editor.

Jackie O, as some of the stations referred to her, had passed away in her sleep at her home in New York City, New York. It was Thursday, May 19, 1994. My editor and friend, J.B. was no longer in this world. Her companion. Maurice Tempelsman was at her bedside when she crossed into her eternal home. Her close friend, Carly Simon was also at her bedside when J.B. passed into paradise. My dear editor friend was not alone at her hour of passing.

Details about J.B.'s life, from her enchanting childhood to her dying breath were reported on every source of media. It seemed the whole world mourned over her death and I, seemingly, was the last one to know about it. I could not even appreciate that the former First Lady of America was my beloved editor. I could only appreciate her understanding, caring witty personality and her intellectually brilliant mind.

The news media reported that J.B. had suffered with a lymphatic cancer called Non-Hodgkin's Lymphoma. It is a blood disease with symptoms of anemia and fatigue. People may experience pain in the abdomen or chest areas. It was there all the time. The shortness of breath I heard when J.B.

spoke. Her feeling exhausted, of which she blamed being overworked. She had wanted to keep her health issues private. I pondered all this information until the day when no one would ever see her beautiful face again. No one would hear that sweet voice speak another word.

J.B. was only sixty-four years old at the time of her death. But she filled her world with as much love as she possibly could and left a positive imprint on the entire world. She will forever live on in people's hearts and in history books for all time.

The day of May 23, 1994, brought more of the misery I was feeling, just like all people around the world. It was the day of J.B.'s funeral. Her children were in attendance at the Arlington Cemetery where their mother was laid to ret beside her first husband, former President, the late John Fitzgerald Kennedy. They now had a place to come visit both of their parents at this place of honor.

I never met J.B. physically. I only knew her in the sense of a long- distance friendship where there was never to be an actual handshake. But yet, both J.B. and I had discussed how fake friendships could be. The so-called friendships of people we had actually met. These were not real in the sense of trust and a lasting bond between two people. This is where I learned that physicality is not a requirement for a true friendship. Never having met J.B. was more than enough proof for me. And I have counted on this lesson learned from her that I have always looked to and referred to as my years have gone by.

As almost everyone else in America, I watched J.B.'s funeral on television. With each station that broadcast it, my heart would sink even deeper as I knew for sure I would never speak to my friend and editor, J.B., ever again. My heart was irrevocably broken as I watched through tears that blurred my vision, numb hands that could not turn the television set off and the ache in my head for the memories of our conversations that came bounding over each other like hot coals in a fireplace.

It was a loss of a dear friend that I cannot explain to this day. A complicated yet simple friendship that did not require or have time for idol worshipping, adornment, or frilly innuendos because neither of us knew the full life story of the other. We were anonymous yet we could identify each other.

Her voice was distinct, and I can recall her every inflection with each of her moods. I knew when she was exasperated with me, knew when she was being compassionate, excited, jubilant, angry and frustrated. And she knew my moods. Happy, nervous, and scared. Yes, our friendship came to that state where we did not have to see each other in the eye to know how one and the other felt. Exactly how a friendship is supposed to be.

I dare anyone to say that J.B. and I did not have a real friendship. All the elements of a true meeting of the minds were there. The only difference is that my friend went on to her eternal home, leaving me here to fend for myself without ever meeting face to face. I will call J.B. my friend until the day that I too will go to my eternal home.

This is the story of how J.B. and I became friends and remained friends, for almost two years before she left this world, and she will forever be J.B. to me.

Epilogue

The story you haver just read is a true account of my conversations with my editor at Doubleday Publishing Company of New York. Her name was Jacqueline Bouvier Kennedy Onassis. She was known to me as J.B. from the very first phone call she made to me regarding my manuscript that I had sent to the Doubleday Publishing Company in New York for review. It was a short self-biography concerning child abuse, murder and witchcraft.

Not once did she ever blame me for the destruction of my childhood. But in her own gracious way of showing compassion, she soothed my insecurities and fears. No other friend since then has been able to accomplish that kind of warmth and understanding.

She taught me how to write the manuscript correctly so it could be fit to be published. And I will forever be grateful to her for all the wisdom she imparted to me.

Here is an excerpt from one of the chapters in which I had a lot of difficulty writing and that only J.B. could carry me through.

....

Conversations with J.B. had immensely guided me on how to display my childhood. Although I did not remember a single moment before the age of four, I am certain it was not as deliberately or cruelly savage as before that age. At least I assume it was a more normal life. Oddly enough my own children have memories they can recall from the age of two or three. How splendid that must be. I would love to have that recall, to see if I had ever experienced a normal childhood at any time. Instead, I had to rely on the memories of my older siblings to fill in the gaps.

My eldest sister would later tell me that my father did not want to bring me home from the hospital after I was born. He wanted to abandon me. My mother had to think twice on whether or not she wanted me at all. This bit of information outright saddened J.B. She attempted to console me.

"Maybe deep within their hearts they knew that you would be the keeper of their sins. How utterly unstable that probably made them. You are still here, still alive for some reason. Do not let that reason be wasted. Instead, be the salvation in spite of it." J.B. forced me to acknowledge the fact that if anyone were to salvage anything memorable from not only my childhood but from my life up to now, it would have to be me.

....

Goodbye J.B. I will forever treasure your friendship

Conversations with Jackie O.

MS Brugetti

Dedication

Dedicated to

Jacqueline Bouvier Kennedy Onassis
K.W. Ostendorf
Anthony Alexander Moreno

If not for them, this book would not be a reality.

Acknowledgements

K.W. Ostendorf.. my Literary Agent

Stephen Miano.... owner That Computer Store, Columbia, SC

Anthony Alexander Moreno .... category content

Prologue

The story you are about to read is a factual account of how I knew Jacqueline Bouvier Kennedy Onassis. The conversations I had with her are still engrained in my memory banks and are still in my heart. She was my editor at Doubleday Publishing Company and beloved friend whom I knew as J.B.

If you are a fan of this wonderful woman then you will be able to see her in the world in which she thrived. A world where celebrity did not exist. Only her life as an editor was relevant at the time that I knew her. There is no fanfare in this book. Only the development from editor to friend.

You will be able to see the warmth, charm, intelligence and sincerity that is Jackie O. If you have had the opportunity to meet J.B., then this will be a further insight as to who she really was outside of the spotlight.

Table of Contents

Made in the USA
Columbia, SC
06 August 2024

39564467R00088